ONE LAST CAST

RADIO

from
Alaska Outdoors Radio Magazine
Evan Swensen

Foreword by Glen Guy (Dusty Sourdough)
Preface by Larry Kaniut

Publication Consultants

PO Box 221974 Anchorage, Alaska 99522-1974

ISBN 1-888125-80-2

Library of Congress Catalog Card Number: 00-105348

Manufactured in the United States of America.

Dedication

One Last Cast is dedicated to Alaska's outdoors, and to Margaret, who allowed me to enjoy working in the wilderness, and for always keeping the home fires burning and a light in the window upon my return.

To: Fran, to may you return to Alaska for one last cast.

Contents

Dedication 3

Acknowledgments 9

Foreword *by Glen Guy (Dusty Sourdough)* 11

Preface *by Larry Kaniut* 11

Introduction 13

Making TV Shows and Videos 16

    The Wrong Reasons 17

    Alone with Bears 19

    Deer Hair Mouse 21

    Horses around Denali 23

    The Kijik Experience 25

    Silver Salmon Derby 27

    Devil's Canyon 29

    George Inlet 31

First Fish 32

    Catch Them Again for the First Time 33

    Alan's First Fish 35

    Diane's First Fish 37

    Jesse's First Fish 39

    Blake's First Fish 41

    Carrie's First Fish 43

    Lars's First Fish 45

    Betty's First Fish 47

    Kathryn's First Fish 49

    Easten's First Fish 51

    Margaret's First Fish 53

857 Charlie 54
  Charlie's *la potage* 55
  Charlie's Dall Sheep 57
  Charlie's Deer 60
  Charlie's Afternoon Moose 63
  Charlie's Parachute Experience 66
  Charlie's Bear 69
  Charlie's Denali Moose 71
  Charlie's Missed Moose *by Ron Eggleston* 73
  Charlie's Four-Moose Day 75
  Charlie's Subsistence Moose 77
  Charlie's Fifth Moose 79
  Charlie's Missing Moose 81
  Charlie's Ghost Moose 84
  Charlie's Prince or Pauper 87
  Charlie's Last Freedom Flight 89
  Charlie's Last Flight 92
Hiking Alaska 94
  Hiking Alaska 95
  City of Trails 96
  Bird Creek Trail 97
  Speechless Brothers 98
  Hiking and Wildlife 101
  Winter Trail 103
  Trent "Lewis and Clark" Clawson 105
  The Final Four 107
Miss Shapen 108
  Miss Shapen One 109
  Miss Shapen 111
  Miss Shapen With the Wow in Her Bow 114
Fishing Alaska 116
  What's a Fish Worth 117
  For Kids Only 119
  Vibes *by Carrie Smith* 121

Top Ten Rivers 123

Two Records 124

Top Ten Lures 125

Volcano Bay Silvers 127

Deer Hair Mouse 130

Fishing Evolution 134

The Fishing Hole 137

Thanks to the Men 139

Take a Kid Fishing 141

Some Things Never Change 143

Rod Holder in the New Boat 145

Rainbow Bay 147

Florette C 149

Florette C Species Specific 151

Florette C Pray for Fish 153

Enid Brown's First Fish on a Fly 156

One in a Row 159

Newhalen River 161

Margaret's Kenai King 163

Mackey Maulers and Dogs 165

Dream Trip 167

Angler's Telegraph 169

Copper River Dip Net 171

Deshka Dardevle 173

Fish Fry 175

Floating and Fishing with Feathers 177

Grand Slam Salmon 180

Grand Slam Salmon 2 183

Listen to the Guide 187

The First Catch and Release 190

Humpies and Halibut 193

Halibut on a Fly 195

Hi-Ho Humpie 197

Homestead to Alaska and Back 199

Hovercraft Kings 201

Iliamna Fishing Competition 203
Buy Him Tad Pollys *by Margaret Swensen* 205
Newspaper Salmon 207
The Real Shore Lunch 209
Closed, Gone Fishing 211
Fly Rod Diplomacy 213
Spring Diggings 215
Turnagain Tide Tragedy 217
Shell's Silvers 219
Alaska Outdoor's Other Side 220
Outdoor's Other Side 221
Alaska for Alaskans 224
Denali for Alaskans 226
Denali Then and Now 229
CAVU 231
Friends, Family, and a Fire 233
Sunken Northwestern 236
Hunting is... 237
Maker of the Moose and Me 239
Mat Valley 241
Max Chickalusion 243
Mush You Huskies 245
Litter 248
Play Together, Stay Together 251
Straight Stretch 253
Take a Kid Hunting 255
Don't Kill the Dream *by Lars Swensen* 257
A Majority of One 259
Enough and to Spare 261
How Is it Really 263
It's Alaska, Not Alaskan 265
Motoring Up Memories *by Lars Swensen* 267
The Last Hunt 269
One Last Cast 272

Acknowledgments

This book was made possible in part due to the friendship and association I've had with a great number of guides, lodge owners, outfitters, and others: Roy and Shannon Randall, Afognak Wilderness Lodge; Ken Robertson, Alaska Drift Boaters; Dianne Debuk, Alaska Saltwater Charters; Herb Eckmann, Alaska Sausage; Bob and Curt Trout, Alaska TroutFitters; Alaska Wilderness Lodge; Ekwok Lodge; Steve Novakovich, Emerald Pines Lodge; Andy Couch, FishTale River Guides; Charlie Warbelow, 40-Mile Air; Mike Gorton, Goodnews River Lodge; Grand Aleutian Hotel; Laurence John, Great Alaska Fish Camp; Greg, Mark, and Sandy Bell, High Adventure Air Charters; Iliamna Lake Resort; Kevin and Cindy Sidlinger, Ishmalof Island Lodge; Martha Sikes, Karluk River Lodge; Craig Ketchum, Ketchum Air Service; Jerry and Karen Pippen, Rainbow Bay Resort; Steve Mahay, Mahay's Riverboat Service; John and Joyce Logan, Skwentna Lodge; Steve and Louise Johnson, Talaview Lodge; Sandy Kellin, Trophy King Lodge; Art Warbelow, Warbelow's Air Ventures; White Mountain Lodge; and numerous guides whose names are mentioned in *One Last Cast*. It has been my privilege to fish, hunt, hike, and recreate with many of Alaska's top guides and best lodges. To these kind people and places I extend my warmest thanks for nearly five decades of the best of Alaska's outdoors.

My heartfelt thanks to the loyal listeners of Alaska Outdoors Radio Magazine. It is your encouragement that kept me writing and delivering each program's *One Last Cast*.

To the authors whose works have been published by Publication Consultants, and your courage and dedication that pointed the way—thank you all!

Foreword
by Glen Guy

It is starting to snow harder as I walk to my little cabin to go to work. I consider myself one of the luckiest guys on earth ... I live in Alaska! Not only do I live in paradise, but in the lifestyle most people can only dream of. My home is a log cabin on the Little Susitna River, as is my small cubby hole I lovingly call "The Studio." When I'm not performing somewhere you can more than likely find me there working on my next book.

I step up on my porch, brushing the snow from my parka, as my ever faithful wolf-dog, Shadow Spirit, charges to my side and unceremoniously shakes the snow from her pure white coat. I brush the snow from me—again, and we go in and start the day's work—if that's what you want to call it.

The morning passes quickly and the words flow smoothly. Dusty once again is in trouble on the Last Frontier and then it happens—uninvited, Murphy shows up, writer's block, or whatever you want to call it; the well goes dry and I run out of words. I lean back in my chair, close my eyes, and am nudged by the wet, cold nose of my furry companion, Shadow Spirit. She wants outside. While she's doing whatever wolf-dogs do, I fix myself a cup of coffee and then turn on my old radio. Just in time I here the announcer's voice say: "Now stay tuned for Alaska Outdoor Magazine." Great! I say out loud and as the commercials run I let Shadow Spirit in and get comfortable to listen to a show for Alaskans by Alaskans.

Evan's guest is a fishing guide giving the latest scoop on ice fishing and he gently asks leading questions that obtain maximum answers of his friend and guide. The hour passes quickly and soon Evan is graciously thanking his guest for coming and saying, "There's just time for one last cast."

One Last Cast was always my favorite part of Evan's show. Sometimes they were hilariously funny stories that Evan's listeners would send in about their Alaska wilderness experience. Some were Evan's life experiences on the Last Frontier with his family and friends when "Alaska was for Alaskans." Some were filled with humor, others were subtle lessons. But whatever they were filled with, they were always filled with the love Evan has for his home—Alaska.

When Evan told me he was writing a book titled *One Last Cast* I could hardly wait for it to get finished. I've had the privilege to read *One Last Cast* before the rest of the world and take it from me, you are in for a real treat. Once again you can go along and share the catch of a child's first fish, fly the pristine skies of Alaska with Charlie and his pilot, and travel the endless trail of the Last Frontier. This is a book for all ages and a must for the true outdoorsman. Before you start reading I suggest you make yourself a bowl of popcorn and settle into your favorite chair. *One Last Cast* takes you back to the Alaska that will never be again.

Who said, "You can't go back!"

Glen Guy (Dusty Sourdough)

Preface
by Larry Kaniut

Evan Swensen loves fishing. And he loves the outdoors. But more than these, Evan loves his family.

His book, *One Last Cast,* reflects his love of Alaska and his philosophy relating to man's need to fully appreciate it. This is a collection of his sign-off stories from Alaska Outdoors, his radio show that aired in Anchorage during the 90s.

The book consists of 7 sections and 120 vignettes of fishing, camping, hiking, hunting, and flying. In addition to stories about people, wild things, and wild places, these delightful pieces capture the rewards of taking children and family to share in the adventure.

One Last Cast strikes a blow for positive fatherhood, for the love of the outing, and for freedom from a bloated and beauracratic government.

Evan's philosophy about savoring and taking care of our environment shines through in stories like: *Horses Around Denali* where he reminds us that it's you that makes the difference; *Alan's First Fish* shows that much of the thrill of the outing is in the going, not necessarily in the getting; *Carrie's First Fish* proclaims "it's nice for a dad to be needed;" and *Miss Shapen* demonstrates that our labor is rewarded.

Along with his love of Nature, Evan addresses his passion for sharing the experience with family and teaching children the right ways afield: *Blake's First Fish* promotes a powerful lesson for adults from a 6-year-old; *Charlie's Dall Sheep* shows that father and son can not only hunt traditionally but also have fun experimenting; and *Charlie's Parachute Experience* portrays positive parent-child relations in going that extra mile for your children and their friends.

Evan's sharp mind and drying ink take us along with him to enjoy the camaraderie with companions, critters, and Creator—great stuff combining ethical and responsible use of the outdoors and a man's love of the wilderness.

One day I was a guest on Evan's radio program. Culminating the show he read *Buy Him Tad Pollys*, an inspirational piece written by his wife Margaret. She described her avid fisherman husband and his passion for rod and reel. Her conclusion stated, "Change him? Never. Some day he will say, 'I love you more than going fishing.' I couldn't ask for more."

I thought it was an excellent piece and requested a copy after the show. Now I don't have to ask Evan for humorous or inspirational stories because he has produced them for all of us to enjoy in *One Last Cast*.

Larry Kaniut

Introduction

Each Alaska Outdoor Radio Magazine program ended with these words, "And now before we close the show, there's just time for one last cast." I'd then deliver a "warm and fuzzy" story about one of my Alaska outdoors experiences. The first last casts were short, but as my confidence grew, and the length of the program expanded, the last casts also matured. I found myself reusing some of them about every two years, refining and polishing them with each use.

I can't speak for the program's listeners, but one last cast became my favorite part of each program. It was always a pleasure to present them and to relive my Alaska outdoor experiences with listeners. Listeners were kind and complimented me, and even asked if I was going to make a book of one last casts. *One Last Cast* is a book because of the program listener's kind encouragement and Margaret's faith that people would buy and read my stories. My only hope is that those who read *One Last Cast* will be as kind as the listeners of Alaska Outdoors Radio Magazine.

Making TV Shows and Videos

The Wrong Reasons

We had just completed our week of making television shows and were waiting around the lodge for our flight back to Anchorage. During the week we'd been treated to the best fishing Alaska has to offer. Each day we'd fly to a remote stream and fish in waters described in colorful brochures designed to attract anglers from around the world.

Some say, "There are two Alaskas to fish—the one residents go to to wet their lines, and the one visitor anglers see." We had been fishing with visitors and filming their adventures for a worldwide television audience. We'd done it all: kings, chum, reds, pinks, rainbows, pike, grayling, and Dolly Varden. As part of the fishing experience we'd been flown to the "Coast" and seen beluga whales by the hundreds. Our pilot-guide had taken us to an extinct volcano, where we landed on the volcano's lake and stepped into the ancient past as we walked on an island in the lake's middle. The rocky island appeared sterile—free from all life, not even evidence of the almost always present seagulls.

As we waited for our winged ride to Anchorage, we discussed our recent Alaska adventures and the fun of filming fish on every cast. As the conversation advanced, a thought was expressed something like this: If you have to catch fish to have a good time, you went fishing for the wrong reasons.

About that time someone asked why we hadn't been to the area's waterfall and filmed and fished in the pool below the falls. No one had mentioned the falls until now. We didn't know anything about them. Upon inquiry, we discovered that an hour-long hike would take us to the falls. Since our air-

plane was tardy and not expected for three hours, we decided to hike to the falls, fish for an hour, and hike back in
time to catch the plane.

The hike to the falls was more like a run, and without movie
paraphernalia, an angler in good shape may be able to make
it in an hour. Our hour hike stretched into an hour and 25
minutes, leaving us only 10 minutes to film and fish. While
the film crew set up their filming gear, I set up my fishing
rod. We were ready at about the same time.

On the first and only cast, I hooked a small grayling who
wanted to be a movie star. I brought the fish to hand and we
filmed the action with the waterfall as a roaring backdrop.
Our setup, film, cast, land, and release process took 10 minutes and we folded up our gear and retraced our hike to the
airport. We had had only enough time to make one cast, and
catch one fish.

Now when you see Alaska Outdoors on television, you'll
notice in the opening scenes a 4-second clip of me fishing in
front of a waterfall, catching a small grayling. At the end of
one of the half-hour programs you'll hear the announcer say,
"There's just time for one last cast." Then you are witness to
the landing and release of a small grayling. There's a roaring
waterfall behind me and soft music playing in the background.

As the scene closes, you'll hear me repeat what has become
almost an Alaska Outdoors' motto, which I learned on the
runway waiting for an airplane, "If you have to catch fish to
have a good time, you went fishing for the wrong reasons."

Alone With Bears

There is one segment of Alaska Outdoors television show that has drawn a great deal of comment. It is the one recording me spending one day and night hiking and camping alone in bear country.

The segment opens with a scene of me parting company with my companions on a float trip. The scene sets the stage for what is to follow by explaining that there is a big bend in the river we're floating and I'm going to take a cross-country hike and meet my fishing buddies the following day as they float the long way around.

Viewers are treated to my visit to an old trapper's cabin which has been ransacked by a bear. The door is smashed in and the cabin's contents are scattered around the cabin floor in total disarray. Cans of commodities have been crushed and punctured by a big bear's jaws and teeth. The bed's mattress lies ripped and soiled among remnants of cooking oil, flour, and other destroyed food. A bear's intrusion into a cabin is akin to any natural disaster.

A lone hiker and camper could easily become terrified after seeing the aftermath of a bear's visit to a cabin, especially if the camper is going to be camping overnight in the dark in a flimsy tent—alone. Bear tracks are shown along the trail and the maker of the tracks is introduced to the audience. Appropriate background music complements the mood of the moment as fear and tension build with the thought of a bear encounter heavy on my mind.

In addition to the scary parts of being alone in bear country, the viewer is shown a beautiful night camping scene along the beach with a full moon overhead reflecting heavenly light across calm water. I'm shown sitting by a warm, comforting fire reflecting on the day's events and dangers that could be lurking just outside of the fires friendly flicker.

Having survived the terrors of the night I'm then shown hiking to the rendezvous point and being reunited with my companions. The segment ends in a happy reunion, but the fear of being alone in bear country is certainly on the mind of those who see the show.

I'm often asked by many who've seen the segment, "Weren't you frightened being out there all alone with the bears and the dark?"

My response to them and you: "I could have been scared, and would have been scared to be alone at night camping in a tent in bear country if my director, assistant director, and sound man, hadn't been filming the show." And if our guide hadn't been there with a big gun.

Deer Hair Mouse

We were filming a segment for Alaska Outdoors television show when I accomplished three, I've-never-done-before things on one pike in a Southwest Alaska lake. It was a windy day. Too windy to fly-fish, too windy to film. I was prepared for big pike with a 9-foot, number nine rod, and a piece of 50-pound monofilament line as leader. Pike were present, but it was far too gusty to throw a fly, and since that was what we were there to film—we couldn't.

The filming crew and I tried to weather the storm by sitting out of the wind behind a high bank. I had never caught a pike, and obviously had not taken one on a fly. In my fly box was a huge deer hair mouse fly I had carried for several years without even a hint of a strike. The longer we stayed behind the bank, the stronger the gusts were and the more restless I became.

More to be doing something than actually fishing, I set up my rod and put on the old deer hair mouse. As I approached the lake's edge I raised the rod as far as I could reach and let the fly act like a kite. The wind caught the bulky body of the mouse and carried it and my fly line for 30 yards. I played the line out as far as it would go until it touched the water. The moment it settled on the surface it was violently attacked by a mouse-hating pike.

I yelled, "Fish on!" as loud as I could, but the wind grabbed my words and sent them sailing unheard across the lake. Battling the old ice age survivor to the lake's edge, I continued yelling for an audience, but the filming crew could not hear me above the wind.

My first pike lay in shallow water among some reeds. I bent over to remove the hook and remembered their sharp teeth. Not wanting to end up as a casualty, I caught the leader 3 feet from the fish's mouth and began to pull the fish to shore. As the line's tension increased, the pike flipped its ugly head from side to side. The motion caused the fish's teeth to act like a buzz saw on my leader. It was severed, and the pike escaped with my deer hair mouse.

I tried to explain to the filming crew what I'd done, but they wouldn't believe me. They just made jokes and I couldn't convince them that I had caught a pike on my big deer hair mouse. I crossed my heart and hoped to die and received only a, "Yeah, sure."

I'm telling you I got my deer hair mouse fly out in a 50-miles-an-hour gale, perhaps the world's singular northern-kite fishing event. It was taken by a hungry pike and I brought him to shore where he escaped with my fly. Honest!

Horses around Denali

It was a bluebird day. Not a cloud in the sky. The kind of a day movie makers dream of. Our film crew was headed for Denali on the Alaska Railroad. The railroad before dome cars and plush seats. We were going to film a wilderness horsepack trip.

As we stepped off the train we immediately recognized our guide and he us. We were the only ones packing camera gear and tripods. He looked like what we'd expect our guide to look like: ten gallon hat, pointed boots, and, of course, he was bowlegged. He looked like a horse wrangler.

He was well prepared and before you could say "road apples" we were getting acquainted with our mounts. Two young ladies accompanied us, Carrie and Alice, and we were going to film their Alaska wilderness horsepacking trip. Neither had experience with horses.

Not knowing cowboys or horses, Alice about died when told her horse's name was Buck. "Buck! I'm supposed to ride Buck?!"

"No! No!" the wrangler said, "It's not what you think. He's as gentle as they come. We call him Buck—short for buckskin. That's his color. Buckskin. He's our best horse and we reserved him for you."

Horses, wrangler, young lady movie stars, and wilderness all cooperated and we "burned film" as they say in Hollywood. We had the makings of an excellent segment for an Alaska Outdoors TV program, but as evening approached, all that changed.

Without warning, unexpected, low, grey clouds burst over the land. The wise wrangler called it a day and started pitching camp. No sooner than he began to break out tents, grub, and cooking gear, it started to snow. Big snowflakes, and lots of them.

The wrangler allowed Carrie and me to ride our mounts aways back down the trail through the snow. It was an exhilarating ride. We wore warm clothes and rainwear and enjoyed the quiet of the wilderness as it turned from fall-brilliance to pure-white. Gone were the sounds and sights of today and we felt like we were riding the range in some western movie.

Returning to camp completed the western movie dream. At the end of our trail we could see our tent through snow-covered trees. A fire was burning and dinner was being cooked over the open flames. The wrangler had a leanto tarp set up over a big sitting log next to the fire. As soon as we arrived we were handed plates loaded with grub: fried potatoes, canned corn, and a perfectly cooked porterhouse steak.

Carrie and I were having about the best Alaska wilderness experience people are allowed. Next to us, sitting on the log facing the fire, sat our assistant director, fresh from California. "Boy, this is grim," he muttered. "This is really grim."

And there you have it. Life in a capsule. And it's all attitude. The snow, the wet, the cold had depleted our friend's spirit, and at the same time had supercharged our wilderness experience. It's all attitude when it comes to wilderness—it's a memory builder both ways. Either it breaks you down or builds you up, but it's the same wilderness—it's you that makes the difference.

The Kijik Experience

Kijik, as we were told, means "at one with nature or at peace with the land." We were making a video comparing the old ways and modern sportfishing. After we'd completed the shooting it was decided we should call the video *The Kijik Experience*.

The video begins with a campfire scene at dusk. Two Alaska Natives are explaining the old ways to a visitor. As they draw pictures in the sand, they tell of how people of the Aleutian Islands and people of the mainland met at Kijik Lake. This was were the two peoples came together. They talk of hunting and fishing and using the land. As they talked, with the flicker of the fire reflecting off their faces, the video takes viewers back in time and shows a young man carving a spearhead and attaching it to a long, slender willow shaft. The scene moves to the edge of Kijik Lake and the young man attempts three times to take a fish with his spear, and is successful on the third try.

Leaving the lake with his catch, he accidentally drops his spearhead in the sand near the lake's edge, and the video fades and returns to the fireside history lesson and slowly evolves into two modern-day anglers fishing with an elder Alaska Native, Macy Hobson. The anglers catch and release their share of fish as they're instructed by their Native elder friend.

They are invited to go with Macy to his fish camp where he teaches them to put out subsistence nets. The net is piled on the back of Macy's boat, which he rows out into the lake. An anchor is dropped, which a line is attached to it and the net. Then Macy returns to shore allowing the net to play off the back of his boat until a long fishing net is hanging in the water suspended by floats.

After a short time, the net is pulled, and a good number of red salmon are caught in the net. As the net is pulled and picked of its fish, Macy explains that some of his catch will go to his smokehouse and some to his drying rack for dog food. "It takes one fish per day per dog for my dog team" Macy tells his visitors.

The visitors are then taken to Macy's drying rack and smokehouse. There they're taught to fillet fish, leaving the fillets connected at the tail, so they can hang it on a drying rack outside or on poles in the smokehouse. They're surprised to learn that the flesh part of the fish goes to the smokehouse for Macy and his family and friends. The bones, with some meat still on them, go on the drying rack for dog food.

When asked by the visitors how dogs could chew the bones and get the meat off without getting bones caught in their mouth or throat, Macy responded that he didn't know, but the dogs know. That's what's important, the dogs know.

As the day of fishing ended and the two visitors followed Macy down the beach, one of the visitors noticed a piece of blackened wood sticking out of the sand. He stopped and pulled it out, revealing a carved spearhead, weathered by time. As the video ends, there are flashbacks of the young native spearing fish and then dropping his spearhead in the sand.

We're left with a warm feeling of the past and present. A feeling of respect for the differences in times, in age, in race. We become one with the land. At peace with nature in Kijik country where people come together—now and anciently. It's the Kijik experience.

Silver Salmon Derby

A few years ago we spent several days in Seward fishing and filming the Silver Salmon Derby. We filmed the whole Salmon Derby experience: folks backing their boats down the ramp and launching them off their trailer. Some forgot to put in the plug a couple of times and there were some tense moments. Outboard motors were occasionally difficult to start and we filmed one frustrated guy beating his contrary motor with the broken starting rope.

One Seward Silver Salmon Derby experience we weren't quick enough to film was a hapless angler, loaded with gear and lunch, who tripped at the top of the walk ramp down to the dock. His pride was about all that was harmed, but he sure scattered gear and groceries down the ramp and out on the dock. A few times we witnessed wind overcoming limited skill as boats were backed into other boats when their captain took his operator's refresher course trying to get his boat out of the harbor and into the open sea. Kids were there fishing off the pier near the cleaning station and catching enough little fish to keep up their interest.

People were there from all over the world; some for the first time, some adding one more Seward Silver Salmon Derby to a string of 20 or 30 previous derbies. There were those who came to meet and talk with friends, others to just be a part of the party, but most came to fish—either from a boat in the bay, or from shore, or even off the dock and breakwater. They came with friends and family, they brought their own boats, and they chartered. It didn't seem to matter how they got there or who they were with. It was just a big fishing party.

One laughing angler brought a big brute of a silver to the

judging station to enter his fish for a prize. It was disqualified. He hadn't met the rules. To be eligible for the contest, fish must be caught with a hook and line. He was laughing because he was fishing just outside the small boat harbor, and his rejected entry had jumped into his boat. Seems there were a lot of jumpers, so he, and others, stopped to fish among the jumping school, and one high-jumping salmon cleared the boat's gunnels and landed on the guy's lap. It made a good story, and probably a good meal, but no prize.

Another angler turned in a 28-pounder, only to discover it was a king, not a silver, and his dream of taking home the money was quickly reduced to two fish fillets.

When you watch the Alaska Outdoors television show about the Seward Silver Salmon Derby, you'll quickly notice that we did more filming than fishing. We spent a week at the derby and never caught a single silver. We were blessed with tom cod, a couple of ling cod, two ugly Irish Lords, and things that grabbed our fishing gear and took it with them. Maybe a shark, sea lion, halibut, or probably the bottom.

When the week was over, the final cannon was fired, and the prizes were handed out, we knew we'd had a good time and had a good program for TV. We'd also proved and strengthened our near-motto: If you have to catch fish to have a good time, you went for the wrong reasons. We must have been at the Seward Silver Salmon Derby for the right reasons. We sure had a good time.

Devil's Canyon

Steve Mahay asked me to produce a movie and video of his attempted run up Devil's Canyon on the Big Susitna River. A few kayakers had successfully navigated down the canyon during a low-water time. A rafter tried the canyon, but was thrown out of his boat and floated the river in his life jacket, barely escaping with his life. Other attempts to go down Devil's Canyon have been frustrated, and some adventurers have paid the ultimate price for their try at the canyon—they were killed.

One brave, but foolish, boat manufacturer tried to take his product up the canyon and was turned back when the canyon's hydraulics sucked his boat under the water, never to be found. He and his crew were plucked from the river by a passing helicopter and saved from their folly.

Then came Steve Mahay, master riverboat operator. Steve watched the canyon and its surging water and decided he would make the attempt and asked Alaska Outdoors to film the results. We agreed on condition we could record the results whether fame or failure.

Steve spent the better part of September modifying his craft, overhauling its powerplant, and contemplating his run at Devil's Canyon. Although September had been a rainy month, a few days before Steve's window of opportunity for the attempt weather cleared, and water levels in the Big Su abated to such a level that Steve felt his boat would have a chance of making the run.

On the day of the attempt, Steve was prepared. He wore a wet suit and crash helmet, hired a helicopter occupied with an experienced rescue worker to fly cover, and filled his boat with flotation material.

Our film crew was also ready for whatever happened. We agreed that our job was to film the event, not get involved with either assisting Steve on his run or participating in a rescue if the attempt turned sour and Steve needed help. We would record the outcome no matter if Steve succeeded, or even lost his life in the attempt.

Filming from strategic points along the route, being placed there by helicopter, we shot the scene as Steve was pounded by waves of rushing water into a solid rock wall, puncturing his boat, but not doing enough damage to stop the run. Cameras rolled film as Steve picked his way through class six rapids where his 50-mile-an-hour boat barely moved, his speed almost matched by the descending river cascading over boulders bigger than Steve's boat. We recorded on film the run around Hotel Rock and up over Heaven's Gate, and finally into the calm water above the canyon.

I met Steve at the end of his run and we shook hands and hugged, grateful that he'd succeeded, and relieved that he'd not been hurt or killed. Barrels of fuel were flown in and Steve continued up the Susitna to the Denali Highway, were he could get his boat out of the water and return to Talkeetna.

The next spring, Steve's film was shown at the Great Alaska Sportsman show and his video was released for purchase. I suspect that if you visit Steve Mahay's Riverboat Service in Talkeetna today, you can meet the only man to take a boat up Devil's Canyon, and he'll probably sell you a copy of his video. It's an exciting video, and although I was there, and filmed the climbing of the canyon, and know Steve made it to the top, there are times shown in the video, that were so very close, when it could have gone either way, I almost expect a Twilight Zone ending and see Steve and his boat sucked under the Su. That's how close Steve came to meeting his Maker—in Devil's Canyon on the big Susitna River at the foot of Denali.

George Inlet

We filmed our guide and his clients pulling a crab pot. The guide told us he was sure it would be full and if it wasn't, the only reason would be that a passing fishing boat robbed it in our absence. When a crab pot is robbed, it is an unwritten rule that the thief replaces the bait and leaves a six-pack for the owner.

When we pulled our pot, we discovered only a couple of small crab. The bait we had placed there had been replaced with new bait. "Damn," said our guide, "our pot has been robbed and the crook didn't even leave a six-pack."

The last two days of our filming saw us catching sea-run silvers. The fishing was spectacular, a grand finale to our summer's shooting. As this was the last shoot, and we were heading home, we decided to keep a few fish for the freezer.

I assisted the guide in putting several big silvers in a box. After packing the box full of fish, I sealed it and wrote my name and address on the top. Then I carried the box of fish to the waiting van and placed it in the back with the rest of my gear. We then left for the Ketchikan Airport in another vehicle followed by the van of fish and gear.

Back in Anchorage, I told my children I'd brought a surprise. We took the box of fish to our freezer and opened it. At either end of the box was a George Inlet beach rock packed in newspaper. Sandwiched between the rocks was a six-pac.

Knowing I am a teetotaler, my children looked at me in dismay. They really became confused when I began to laugh. It took a minute before I could stop laughing enough to tell them about the crab-pot-robber tradition of Southeast Alaska.

I've never admitted the joke to either the guide or my shooting crew. But some day, some way, I'll get even.

First Fish

Catch Them Again
for the First Time

Do you remember your first fish? Of course you do. I remember mine like it was last week. I was in Oak Creek canyon on opening day, fishing with a 10-foot cane pole, no reel, a piece of line tied to one end, and night crawlers for bait. I have relived the innocent excitement of that moment as I have witnessed my children catch their first fish.

Alan was fishing from our homemade 12-foot boat rightly christened Miss Shapen. It was early morning and patches of ground fog blocked the rising sun, putting a chill in the spring air when his first fish, a Swanson River rainbow, took the single egg and retreated to cover only to be turned and boated.

Diane and Blake went from spectator to angler with a Russian River red. Diane's was wrapped in foil, placed under campfire coals and became the day's lunch. Blake's battle ended with the release of a foul-hooked fish.

Jesse got hooked on fishing sitting on my shoulders. He wasn't big enough for his own hip boots so he used mine, with me still in them. He caught a greater number of Otto Lake grayling than his limited knowledge of math permitted him to count. A couple of them made breakfast in the camp frying pan. The rest were released to thrill another.

Carrie became an official angler on the spit at English Bay. She was fishing in salt water when a 14-inch Dolly took her bait. Her method of playing and landing was backing up the beach while hollering her lungs out for Dad's help.

Lars broke into the ranks of fishermen on two different Talachulitna River species—pinks and grayling, and on a fly rod. He was having pretty good luck while fishing for pinks on the Talachulitna River. We ate his catch.

Betty's first fish was a silver. She was fishing with fishing guide Steve Mahay from the back of his boat on one of his secret backwater sloughs off the Big Susitna River.

Kathryn's first fish came to her not too far from where Betty landed her silver. She was fishing for silvers and caught some later in the day. Her first fish, however, was a Dolly Varden. She was pleased about it, and about the fact she outfished her dad for the day.

My youngest son Easten was a ten-year old Webelo boy scout when he landed his first fishing with his older brother, Lars. The excitement of the two brothers returning home with stories of a mess of fish landed and released will long be remembered.

There is magic in fishing and a person's first catch, and it continues for a lifetime. The real magic is that the first time can be relived with emphasis by sharing another's first fish and especially if the other person is a youngster who could not have the experience without your help. As with us all, we'll remember the first one and be eternally grateful to the person who helped us catch it.

Alan's First Fish

Miss Shapen was constructed for the sole purpose of taking her builders fishing on the Swanson River. And fishing we did. It was from the deck of Miss Shapen that my oldest son Alan took his first fish. It was early spring in the second year of Miss Shapen's life and Alan was four years old when he and I took the little boat with a wow in the bow and camped and fished along the Swanson.

Alan may not even remember the day, but I do. We had waited all winter and watched the snow pile up on the bottom of Miss Shapen lying upside down in the backyard. When weather turned warmer we assisted the snowmelt by shoveling the compacted white stuff off and away from Miss Shapen. Toward spring, as increasing daylight hours allowed a sliver of sunlight between job and dinner, we'd temporarily tip Miss Shapen on her side and do little repairs and maintenance and talk and dream of the season's first fishing trip.

Then the fateful Friday found us motoring down the Seward Highway in our old Nash Rambler with Miss Shapen on top. It was nearly dark when we showed up at the Swanson. It was dark by the time the tent was pitched, sleeping bags spread out, dinner prepared and consumed, and the 5-horsepower Evenrude mounted on Miss Shapen's sloped transom in anticipation of the morning's first light and the season's first cast.

Alan hardly slept that night. It was his first real trip away from his mother, away from the security of his own bed, and then there was the excitement of being big enough to go upriver and fish with his dad. Every time I'd check my watch during the night, he'd be awake and ask if it was time to go fishing yet.

Finally it was time to fish and we pointed Miss Shapen upriver pushed by our little, blue-gray outboard blowing a bluish exhaust cloud. There was a spring chill to the air, and, although the Evenrude was incapable of putting Miss Shapen on the step, the small breeze created by our upriver movement bit our cheeks and nose. Realizing that if Alan got too cold it might spoil his trip and even turn him off future fishing outings, we stopped at the first upriver hole.

I'd never fished that hole before, thinking that it was too close to the road to be very good fishing. Alan was fishing with a packaged combination outfit purchased from B and J Surplus. I baited his number 14 gold hook with a small yellow salmon egg. After a few tries he was casting in the Swanson the way we had practiced it back home in the front room.

It was on maybe his fourth or fifth try that a small Swanson rainbow grabbed the hook and ran for cover. Alan took two steps back and at the same time jerked with all his 4-year-old might. The momentum of the motion caused him to stumble over the tackle box, scattering hooks, leader, line, and lures. He quickly recovered and discovered he had landed his first fish.

Having heard us talk about releasing the little ones, he immediately asked if this one was big enough to keep and take home and show mom and then eat. If it wasn't at least 8 inches, we always threw them back, even if we were fishing for a shore lunch or campside breakfast. I showed Alan the tape measure where it read 8 inches. He put his fish alongside the tape. The fish was too short. Then Alan did what every sportsman has done forever; he released his fish. The little rainbow darted for the protection of the overhanging bank.

That's how I remember Alan's first fish. We've fished and hunted together now for nearly four decades and Alan still has that kind of personal integrity. If it ain't right he just doesn't do it. I've always been grateful for Swanson River, the little boat with the wow in the bow, for fishing, and for the opportunity to be one on one with my son and being there when the 4-year-old took a giant step toward the man he was to become.

Diane's First Fish

You often hear me recommend that when you go fishing, take a kid with you. When I say kid, I mean either boy or girl. Some of my best times on the fishing stream have been with my daughters. Diane became acquainted with hiking in the outdoors before she could walk. Right from birth she seemed to have a special feeling for wilderness and wildlife and found fun walking through the woods on Dad's shoulders or standing in a pack on Dad's back.

She was nearly four when she joined me and her older brother for a fishing outing on the Russian River. There wasn't a campground established then. The campground and trails came later. We found the Russian by parking our car just before the road to Kenai crossed the river from where the road and the peninsula get their names.

There was somewhat of a trail to the river, but as in most fishing holes, the good fishing was on the other side of the river. Diane carried her own pack loaded with gear and goodies equal to her strength and ability to pack. She tired quickly but kept going with the encouragement of big brother and occasionally holding Dad's hand.

When we came to the river she didn't hesitate to jump on Dad's back for the piggyback ferry trip across the Russian. Once on the other side the hole quickly was located where the fish were holding.

Before fishing gear was set up we built a small fire ring with rocks and started a campfire in anticipation of catching a fish. Once the fire was going we got the gear out and started casting. Seems like Diane needed help with her cast as her short legs and inexperience left her lure short of the fish.

With help from Dad she was soon playing a tail-walking red. The fish was hooked good and the angels assigned to watch over little girls who fish did their jobs as Diane was able to bring the Russian River red to shore where I could help her land her first fish.

The fish was quickly dispatched and cleaned. Then it was wrapped in foil and placed beneath the coals of our fire. A few more sticks of wood were added to the fire and we went back to fishing.

Not long later, when hunger twitched our bellies, we returned to the fire and retrieved Diane's first fish. We placed the fish on a nearby log and unwrapped the foil covering. We took a fork from our packs, and when the skin was peeled from the cooked red we dug in community style. We were filled before the fish ran out and we left it on the log, returning periodically for nibbles and snacks.

Since that day I've eaten a good many shore lunches, some prepared by guides with great cooking skills and served on the riverbank with flair, on fresh linen tablecloths and the lodge's finest china. But none have left me with a finer memory than the one on the bank of the Russian and the simple lunch of Diane's first fish.

Jesse's First Fish

Kids don't care if it's in a plane, a boat, or just the family clunker. Jesse for example. When he was barely three he and I took our old converted camper Corvan and went fishing.

A Corvan was Corvair's minivan. Both the Corvair and Corvan are extinct, but back in scatty-eight we owned one that became our ride to Alaska's outdoors for several years.

We got our Corvan cheap. The rear engine had caught fire and burned too much to repair, so the owners gave it to our family if we could fix it and make it run. We located a new engine Alaska Sales and Service was happy to part with for about their cost. We put it in the Corvan ourselves.

The Corvan had been a delivery vehicle so we built seats, beds, cooking counter, and table in the back. We put in a propane cooking range, propane heater, and propane lights. A hole was cut in the Corvan's side over the table, and another one in the door opposite, and we put a travel trailer type window in each hole.

Our kids were small back then and with bunk beds over the rear engine compartment, the table lowered, and one person sleeping on the cooking counter, and another on the front seat, we could sleep six or eight depending on the ages of those with us.

Jesse and I left the rest of the family engaged in other activities and just the two of us headed for Otto Lake near Healy. Our Otto Lake experience was way before the Parks Highway was constructed, perhaps even conceived. Business had me engaged for a few days at Usibelli Coal Mine and so the family decided to join me and camp along the way in our Corvan and duplex 9-by-12 tent.

One of Usibelli's coal truck drivers told me about Otto Lake, said it had a bunch of small grayling in it. Jesse and I decided to test it. Fish were jumping when we arrived and we quickly set up our gear. We noticed the fish were jumping, but jumping out in the lake farther than we could cast, especially Jesse.

I put on my hip boots, lifted Jesse to my shoulders, and started wading toward the jumping fish. The lake was shallow and we waded where we could easily cast to the fish— even Jesse could reach them. He'd cast to the right and I to the left. More often than not we had doubles on—mostly catch and release—not because of fishing philosophy; the grayling were just too darn small. For a 4-year-old sitting on Dad's shoulders, it was fishing heaven.

Finally a few respectable enough for breakfast were kept. When my shoulders gave out we returned to the Corvan and then to camp. Breakfast was special for Jesse as he had been the proud provider.

The Corvan's gone, Jesse grew up and now takes his own children to the outdoors. I don't know how much he remembers about the Otto Lake grayling, the Corvan, or fishing from Dad's shoulders, but in my mind, I remember. It's a good memory. One that I wouldn't have had, had I not taken the kid fishing.

Blake's First Fish

Russian River is one of my favorite fishing holes. Of the ones you can drive to, my favorite. Sure it's crowded during the red-salmon run, but that's part of the fun.

After the red run winds up, and most anglers put away their equipment or go elsewhere, the Russian becomes a super rainbow and Dolly stream, and one of the prettiest. When most fishermen think of the Russian, they think of crowds, but not in September, October, and even until snow and cold makes it too unpleasant to fish.

When the reds are in, we mostly fish the Russian from eight or nine o'clock in the evening until the first ferry brings new anglers the following morning. I say we fish the Russian, but not really—we fish the Kenai just below where the Russian joins the bigger river.

That's what we were doing the night Blake took his first fish. We arrived late in the evening and took the last ferry across the Kenai. There were a few hardy anglers who stayed on the Russian side when the ferry departed for its last trip of the day, and we joined them in search of salmon.

We discovered from talking to those who remained, and those who took the ferry back, that fishing had been rather poor throughout the day. Blake and I started to cast, but not with a great deal of enthusiasm. He was perhaps six at the time and soon tired when no fish immediately accepted his offering. We decided to take an early lunch break and give the fish a chance to calm down from the all-day marathon they'd been running trying to get up the Russian past the horde of fishermen, now departed. The diehards, those anglers who'd stayed over, continued to fish, but with no better success than Blake and I had with our lines out of the water and eating Mom's meatloaf sandwiches and oatmeal cookies.

About the time the lunch ran out, I noticed a group of reds had moved into the hole Blake and I had been fishing earlier. "Get your gear," I whispered to Blake, "There's some fish in our hole."

Blake picked up his rod and I left mine on the bank. By me standing in the swift current just above Blake, and stopping some of the water pressure, he was able to safely wade out in his short 6-year-old-size boots far enough to cast to the fish. It only took him a couple of tries and then bam, he had a red on. In the half-light of the evening we could see the fish jump and twist and turn trying to throw the hook.

Blake soon had an audience. Almost all those fishing laid down their rods and became Blake's cheering section. One angler grabbed his net and stepped into the river below Blake. "Bring him in and I'll net him for you," he said.

Blake was able to bring the fish near enough for the kind angler to reach out and net Blake's catch. When the fish was brought in, the cheering section moved around the net to take a look. It was then discovered that the fish had been hooked behind the head.

"Foul-hooked," someone said.

And then another piped in, looking at the 6-year-old now holding the net, "It's alright kid, you're little. Keep the fish. We don't care and nobody's going to say anything." One man took the hook out for Blake and left the fish in the net.

Blake looked at me with questioning eyes. "What do I do?" he asked.

"It's your fish," I said.

"Isn't it against the law?" Blake asked.

"Yes, it is."

"It's alright," the crowd chipped in. "Don't worry. Go ahead and keep your fish."

Blake looked at me and then at the crowd. He took the net and turned it upside down and let the fish go back in the water.

The now quiet crowd returned to their fishing. A new run of reds came in and most folks caught at least one fish. Any that were foul-hooked, were released.

Carrie's First Fish

Carrie became an official angler on the spit at English Bay. She was fishing in salt water when a 14-inch Dolly took her bait.

English Bay is a short flight from Homer. The airport, such as it is, is a wide, flat, narrow strip of gravel on the spit separating the ocean from the brackish lagoon. When the tide's out, the lagoon's almost empty except for the clear-water stream running through its middle surrounded by mud and slick moss. There's a rock cliff at one end of the airstrip. The town's church, complete with a short steeple at one end and a chimney at the other, sits on a small hill at the approach end of what locals call English Bay International Airport.

Fortunately, prevailing winds allow landing over the church, keeping the wings between steeple and chimney, slipping the aircraft on final approach, and immediately dropping flaps and standing on the brakes as soon as wheels feel gravel. If the pilot isn't lined up right, he can go around.

Coming in from the other direction would mean coming in low over the ocean, swinging in front of the cliff at the last moment, just before touchdown. There's no chance to go around. If the plane is going too fast or is too high, the church hill and church at the other end of the strip will wear a bended prop and twisted wings. There's not many attempts at a landing from the cliff end of English Bay International Airport.

The day Carrie caught her first fish found us approaching English Bay in our old Stinson Voyager model 108-3. I keyed the radio mike and made a blind announcement advising any traffic in the area that 857 Charlie was about to land. Coming over the church at 64 miles an hour, and with the cliff looming at the other end, makes the landing seem more dangerous than it really is. We touched down, dropped the flaps, hit the brakes, and stopped way short of the runway's end.

The tide was out, but was just turning, as we had anticipated. We parked 857 Charlie and unloaded our gear. A couple of locals came down from town and checked us out and gave a current fishing report.

We decided to fish the salt water on the incoming tide. The locals told us that they had been doing good on Dollies. Carrie's rod was the first one out of the plane and it was soon set up ready to fish with. Carrie took her rod and was soon casting into the almost lake-like calm water of the bay.

Before I could get my rod up and running, I heard this gosh-awful scream coming from the beach. I didn't know Carrie could make that much noise.

"Help, Dad! Help!" she screamed. I ran to her side only to discover she had hooked into a feisty sea-run Dolly that had taken exception to being caught by a little girl and was doing its best to keep its tail in the ocean.

Carrie's line and rod were set up for reds up the river we intended to go fishing after the tide brought in the next run. She was way over-geared for this little Dolly she was making a fuss over. The Dolly never stood a chance. It was well hooked and Carrie's method of playing and landing was backing up the beach while hollering her lungs out for Dad's help. She soon succeeded in beaching the fish and held it and her salmon rod up for a family album photograph.

I can't remember if she released her Dolly or kept it for breakfast. I hardly remember going up the stream catching reds. I don't remember the takeoff toward the cliff or the flight home. But I've got the picture in our family scrapbook of Carrie standing on the beach at English Bay holding up her first fish. And, I'll never forget Carrie hollering for Dad's help. It's nice for a dad to be needed.

Lars's First Fish

Talachulitna River is a unique stream. It's less than an hour's flight from Anchorage in a small plane; it's crystal clear; almost all of it is wadable for fly-fishermen; all five species of Pacific salmon run its waters, and it has an excellent rainbow, grayling, and Dolly fishery. The rainbow fishery is enhanced due to its catch-and-release policy.

I've fished the Tal hundreds of times and have never tired of its beauty and its fish. Nearly all my children have wet their lines in the Tal, always with success and satisfaction.

And so it was with Lars. Lars and I were on our way to a sheep hunt in the Alaska Range when he took his first fish in the Tal. We hadn't planned to fish; we planned to meet our pilot on the airstrip servicing Talaview Lodge. Mark Miller, our pilot, was weathered out, so Lars and I took to fishing while waiting, and then ended up spending the night.

Steve Johnson, manager of Talaview Lodge furnished us gear and got Lars started on a fly rod. Lars took to fly-fishing like kings take to the Tal. It wasn't long and he was having pretty good luck on pinks that infested the Talachulitna River. He was hooking them but was unable to bring one to shore. He would get close enough to touch the fish and then it would dash off to deep, swift water and escape the hook.

Casting to a group of fish moving slowly upriver along the opposite bank, he was surprised when he hooked a grayling. So surprised that he tripped, or slipped, on a boulder and went in over his hip boots. Recovering from the fall, he proudly stood with boots full of river water and excitedly exclaimed, "Dad I still got him, I still got him."

And, indeed he still had him, and he kept him. Throughout the afternoon and late evening, Lars continued developing his fly-fishing skills on pink salmon, releasing them all, and keeping his feet underneath him and his boots dry.

The next morning, while waiting for Mark and our ride to our chosen hunting area, we ate Lars's grayling catch for breakfast.

Lars has fished a good number of different spots in Alaska and makes the claim that he's never been skunked—and I believe him. We've pushed both ends of the season and Lars always manages to catch at least one fish. I don't know whether he's just real lucky, blessed by fish deity, or if it's Steve Johnson's, Talachulitna River fly-fishing lessons, but Lars outfishes me every time. But isn't that what a dad is supposed to do? Teach the kid to be better than the dad. Seems to me if the kid isn't better than the dad, one or both of them failed. Following that logic, we're both winners.

Betty's First Fish

The Talkeetna river runs toward the ocean at the foot of Mt. McKinley, North America's tallest mountain. It's not climbers that rush to Talkeetna village, located at the river's mouth, each fall. The climbing is done in the spring. Those, like my daughter and I, who show up in August, suffer from silver fever.

Long before Betty and I used fishing as an excuse for a daddy-daughter date, the Tanaina Indians fished the river for survival, and named it Talkeetna—river of plenty. Talkeetna is a tourist town. Tourism in Talkeetna in August means fishing. Located at the confluence of the Susitna, Chulitna, and Talkeetna Rivers, its location permits access to more than 200 river miles of prime fishing territory. The region boasts the second-largest run of migrating salmon in the world, second only to the Iliamna-Bristol Bay area.

It is two and one half hours by paved highway from our driveway in Anchorage to the boat landing in Talkeetna. The community exists because of good highway access, beautiful scenery along the roadway, specifically the opportunity to see and photograph Mt. McKinley, and fishing. In season, all five species of Pacific salmon frequent these waters. In addition, rainbow trout, Dolly Varden, and grayling can be taken.

On the last Friday before school started one fall, Betty began bugging me about going fishing. She gave me a hug and told me how good a father I was. One hundred and fifty minutes later we were in Talkeetna, registering as guests at the Swiss Alaska Inn for the night, and making reservations with Mahay's Riverboat Service for silver hunting next morning.

Betty talked nonstop during dinner. She changed the subject after every breath. I got the lowdown on everything. Music and musicians. Boys and brothers. Sisters, school, and summer. Clothes, cars, crystal, and charge cards.

We were at the boat landing at eight next morning. Steve Mahay uses jet-powered riverboats for transportation to the clear-water salmon-spawning streams entering the Talkeetna. A 20-minute boat ride weaving between islands and eddies puts us at our private fishing hole, a side stream entering the glacier-fed opaque Talkeetna.

Often silvers will be seen jumping, trying to shed sea lice, or loosen eggs, or for whatever strange urge besets them. That day the surface of the creek was unusually quiet.

In typical guide style, Steve started his, "You-should-have-been-here-yesterday" story as he rigged up the rods. After ten no-nothing casts apiece, we began our own story. "It doesn't matter if we catch fish, it's just being here that's important." Neither guide nor clients need have bothered with the excuses.

Luck changed. Beginning with Betty hooking up first, a serial of fish-capades played throughout the day. Silvers are the most acrobatic of salmon—resembling the jumping, tail-walking, skydiving antics of their cousins—rainbow trout. Every dive, jump, and run trick pulled by a fish brought rock opera audience-like squeals from the teenage angler. It is amazing how the sound exploding from the lungs of a teenage daughter can affect a father. In front of the family room television set it is irritating. On the riverbank, exhilarating. Heard above the stereo, exasperating. Under birch trees, next to mountains, at the end of a fishing rod, like the voice of an angel.

How many fish were caught (some kept, some released), has been lost to history. Numbers are insignificant. What seems to be important is the closeness I felt with my daughter. Sunday afternoon, back home, during a fresh silver salmon dinner Betty confessed, "It really isn't necessary to catch fish to have fun. What is important is that every chance you get, take your dad fishing."

Kathryn's First Fish

Steve Mahay was thinking about operating a lodge at the confluence of Clear Creek and Talkeetna River. The lodge was established, and Steve would be taking it over from the owners who had not been able to make a go of it. Steve invited me to come up and check it out with him. "And we can do a bit of fishing," he said. I explained to Steve that I had made a daddy-daughter date with my daughter, Kathryn, and as much as I was tempted by his invitation, I couldn't come. "Maybe later."

"How about making your daddy-daughter date a fishing trip on the Talkeetna?" Steve questioned. "Bring her along."

And so it was that Kathryn and I found ourselves as the only guests at Clear Creek Lodge and Steve Mahay's sole clients for a two-day-one-night fishing trip. It was late in the season, past the prime silver salmon fishing season, but Dollies and rainbow fishing was just heating up. Once silver fishing quiets down, not many anglers fish the Talkeetna, but, as on many Alaska streams, the real fishing just begins if you're into fishing rather than filling the freezer.

Steve treated us like royalty and we ate the foods of kings and the rich. After dinner we strolled hand in hand along the lodge's paths, pausing to inspect flowers, rocks, and anything else that caught our fancy. But mostly just talking and being a dad and daughter without an agenda.

Later in the evening we sat around the fireplace in the main sitting room and swapped fishing lies with Steve. Steve, always the gentleman, included Kathryn in the conversation and made her feel as important to him as he knew she was to me. When we finally tired, we trundled off to our private rooms for a night's rest to prepare for the next day's fishing.

As we left the lodge next morning Steve asked Kathryn if she'd like to catch a silver if he could find one not too far from where he had guided Betty, Kathryn's sister, several years before. Kathryn agreed.

Steve continued to cater to Kathryn and helped her with gear and bait, and together they fished for silvers. As I remember it, Kathryn was fishing for silvers when this little Dolly thought it was much bigger than he really was and attacked Kathryn's lure like a lunker.

Kathryn kept her composure and landed the little thing, let Steve release it, and then went back to fishing. Throughout the day Kathryn caught more Dollies, a few rainbow, and even landed a couple of fall silvers.

I wasn't keeping track of those things, but I guess Kathryn was, because on the way back home she reminded me that she had outfished her dad and remembered that not only had she caught the most and the biggest, but the first—the little Dolly Varden.

She was pleased about it, and the fact that she outfished her dad for the day. She wrote a couple of paragraphs in her journal about her feelings and appropriately called it "My Dolly and My Daddy."

Kathryn's now a grown-up lady. She no longer walks along lodge paths hand in hand with her dad. She goes to the woods and waters with her husband. But I hope she still remembers our daddy-daughter date and the Dolly that was her first fish.

Easten's First Fish

My youngest son Easten was a 10-year-old Webelo boy scout when he landed his first fish. Just after the snow melted and before the ice was off the lakes I spent an afternoon on the front lawn with his den teaching them to cast a fly rod. Easten and I practiced together a few more times after that and he became a pretty good caster.

I was telling book author and fly-fishing guru Dan Heiner about Easten's success at casting a fly. Dan asked what kind of gear Easten was using. "Oh, some of my old things that he can't get in too much trouble with." Not long after, Dan asked me to stop by his house. He needed my help. And then he added, "Why don't you bring Easten with you; I've got something I'd like to show him."

A few days later found Easten and me in Dan's den which looks something like the fly-fishing department at Mountain View Sports. Dan talked fly-fishing with Easten for a time and then handed him a brand-new rod Dan had just received from Cabella's, an 8-weight, 9-foot, graphite beauty. They talked about the merits of the rod and how it felt in the hand. It was lovely and I could tell Dan thought it was about the best 8-weight rod in his den.

After a few minutes of false casting and passing the rod back and forth Dan handed it to Easten with a comment something like this, "I got this rod just for you. I wanted you to start out fly-fishing with the best."

Easten couldn't believe what he was hearing, but he remembered his manners and thanked Dan gratefully for the gift.

A few days after receiving his gift rod, Easten bought his

own reel. Not quite the same class as the rod, but serviceable nevertheless. Easten continued his front-lawn casting and practice and then the ice went out of Green Lake. Easten's older brother, Lars, invited him to put his fishing lessons and practice to practical application and try out the new rod.

The excitement of the two brothers returning home with stories of a mess of fish landed and released will long be remembered. They became the family entertainment for the afternoon, laughing and kidding each other about the day's events: the fish that actually jumped out of the lake onto the beach in search of Easten's fishing fly, Easten setting the hook so hard on a small one the fish came out of the water and hit him in the chest, and on and on.

Easten still fishes with Dan's gift rod. Dan's generosity, mingled with Easten's natural good heart, has helped Easten become a kind, helpful, considerate young man. Thanks, Dan. You gave Easten more than just a fly-fishing rod.

Margaret's First Fish

Margaret and I honeymooned on Nez Perce Creek in Yellowstone Park. We camped in the exact spot where, years earlier as a boy scout, I had pitched my tent and earned merit badges. My new bride celebrated catching a husband by landing the first, most, and biggest fish. Like all fishermen who carried the day, she rubbed it in. My retort to her needling was, "I'll never take you fishing again." Over the years I've almost kept that threat. Not on purpose, but by default.

In the early years of our marriage we kept close to home with only a few days out each summer. Then babies began arriving. When I was fishing with the older ones, Margaret was at the tent tending the newest arrival. We camped and fished a lot, but Margaret spent a lot of time looking after little ones. We joked about me not taking her again because she outfished me on our honeymoon. It got to be the family tradition. "Don't catch more than Dad. Be sure and let Dad catch the first one. I'm sure Dad's 12-pound silver is bigger than my 17-pounder," was repeated many times in jest. Mom kept fueling the issue by claiming her absence from the water was because of the honeymoon humiliation. Fact is Mom would rather tend babies at home than in a boat or on the bank.

The babies have grown up with families of their own. Married children now take their own children fishing and build their own family traditions. Margaret and I take to the outdoors alone, together, but she's wiser now. She never admits to outfishing me.

857 Charlie

Charlie's *la potage*

 T hree of my sons and I used our old Stinson Voyager Station Wagon, 1948 vintage airplane, to get us to the beginning of our hike off the Nebesna Glacier. We carefully picked our landing spot on the glacier, one we had thoroughly investigated, and landed without incident. Upon landing we turned the plane into the prevailing wind and tied the old bird down with strong ropes, using mountaineer's 18 - inch ice augers for tie-downs. Satisfying ourselves that the plane was safe, we began our weeklong trek to circle Mt. Gordon.

We were traveling light, with just enough food for our allotted time. Our packs, including all camping gear and food, weighed less than 28 pounds each. Our diet consisted of trail mix and chea seed. We did not intend to have a fire. As a safety precaution we made an airdrop of military C rations off a snowfield at the base of the mountain.

We had a delightful trip, never spending a night in the same place twice. Each day we would pack up and go where our instincts directed and then pitch camp where night found us. Weather was typical. Periods of blue sky and sun mixed with times of wind, rain, and even snow.

When we reached our airdrop food cache we were ready for a change of menu. Even C rations sounded good, so good we decide to mix them all together in the only pan we had. In went wieners and beans, beef stew, spaghetti, and several other items peculiar to C rations. The concoction, under the circumstances, was edible, if not tasty, and it was hot. To this day when a conversation turns to hiking one of us will ask, "Do you guys remember Mt. Gordon *la potage?*"

When we returned to our airplane we received a surprise.

During our absence the glacier had melted more than 18 inches. Our ice auger tie-downs were lying on top of the glacier. We do not know how long it took for the glacier to melt enough to free our anchors, but if the wind had come up it would have blown our transportation over the edge of the glacier where it would have rolled up into a little red ball at the bottom of a crevasse. We have yet to discover a safe way to tie an airplane down on a glacier for an extended time.

Charlie's Dall Sheep

Charlie's pilot, guiding Charlie in a circling pattern over Nebesna Glacier, watched as Pettijohn greased the little Champ onto the glacier's icy back. Charlie's pilot continued to circle while the Champ taxied to the glacier's side and Pettijohn confirmed that it was safe to land the 1948 Stinson by following the same route the Champ had taken. Nebesna Glacier's makeshift airport, a narrow ribbon of smooth ice, was just below Mt. Gordon's 9,000-foot summit in Alaska's Wrangell Mountains at a time when Alaska was still for Alaskans. Before Washington D.C. locked up the land for the personal benefit of National Park Service rangers.

After landing, and tying Charlie down using mountain climber's 18-inch ice augers as anchors for the tiedown ropes, a base camp was established on sandbar-like glacier moraine between Nebesna Glacier's ice and lush underbrush growing to the edge of the moraine. Across the glacier lay Orange Hill's abandoned gold mine, depriving the occupants of the two airplanes the sense of being the first to walk the wild land at the foot of Mt. Gordon. Other than the noise of making camp by the recently arrived people, the silence of wilderness was only stirred by an occasional low grumble from Nebesna as the river of ice shifted and slipped in its eternal slide to extinction.

As the late August sun slipped behind Mt. Gordon Charlie and Champ's people dined on dinner prepared over their one-burner camp stove. It would be the last hot meal they'd enjoy for five days. Anticipating their return, the campers heated water in a large pan, stirred in the recommended amount of strawberry Jello, and placed the lid-covered pan in an alcove next to Nebesna's icy wall. Experience told the camp's older sheep hunters that a cold Jello treat would be a welcome indulgence after five days of chea seed and gorp.

During the night, wicked winds from Prince William Sound found their way over the Wrangells and whipped down Nebesna's exposed back. With the arrival of morning, the wind slipped away as dawn's first light allowed Charlie's and Champ's pilots to check on their little birds still tethered to million-year-old ice. The birds were safe and the ice augers were screwed down a little tighter, taking up the slack created by the night's wind and mildly melting ice. The only casualty, and only a minor one, was that black sand from the moraine had been lifted by the wind and deposited in ample amounts over and in the hunter's gear.

By the time the sun crested distant peaks the hunters were well on their way toward Dall sheep land on the other side of Mt. Gordon. Charlie's pilot and Alan, his oldest son, were on their first sheep hunt. For the next five days they wandered the slopes of Mt. Gordon in pursuit of a white ram, but none meeting their definition of trophy crossed their path. In late afternoon of the fifth day they began their descent to Charlie for the return flight to Anchorage and home.

About halfway down Mt. Gordon the two hunters made camp and spent the night. Arising early, Charlie's pilot, not yet clothed and with the effects of the night's sleep still restricting proper vision, opened the tent door. Thirty yards away, framed by the outline of the rainfly, stood a trophy ram silhouetted against dawn's dark-blue sky. Charlie's Pilot's son was rudely awakened as the invention of John Browning boomed from within the tent awning and the big ram completed his life's mission.

It was nearly noon before the hunters had completed the tasks of dressing their animal and caping the trophy. Far below they could see three small sheep wander onto a small plateau just before the open area of the mountain turned into alders and brush. By the time the hunters had finished taking care of their trophy and packed up their camp, the three sheep below had fed to their fill and were lying down in the sun on the open plateau.

As the hunters, still in their white sheep-hunting clothes,

approached from above, from where few enemies of sheep approach, the sheep offered no fear or gave any indication that they were disturbed by the hunters' presence. Even when the hunters arrived within 300 yards, the animals did not feel inclined to flee. Alan decided to test the theory that sheep have no fear if approached from above by something white and not in a hurry. He took off his pack, got down on his hands and knees, and began traversing the hill in a slow, deliberate manner, much like a grazing sheep would do. He moved to the right for about 30 yards and then back left 30 yards; each time moving a few feet forward toward the reclining sheep. After nearly an hour Alan had moved to within 30 feet of where the sheep were resting.

As the distance closed between Alan and the sheep, the animals began to show some sign of being nervous and one of them stood up and stared at Alan. Alan had learned not to look them in the eye so he did not return the stare, but pretended to look elsewhere. The sheep was on alert, but did not make a motion to move. Alan moved a step or two closer. The other two sheep stood and stared. Alan slowly rose on his feet to a football lineman's stance, still not looking directly at the sheep.

Finally the sheep's curiosity got the best of them and one took a step forward, and then another also took a timid step. All at once Alan charged into the small half-circle of standing sheep, nearly touching them as they bolted and fled. Alan knew pursuit was impossible, even if he had wanted to join in the chase. He had accomplished what he had intended to find out. As far as Alan is concerned, given the right set of circumstances, if required, a hunter in a desperate situation could take an Alaska wild sheep with a spear.

Charlie's Deer

Montague Island is the land barrier between the vast Pacific Ocean and Prince William Sound. Had we voyaged with Captain James Cook we'd have taken our leave of Alaska from Montague Island when we started our trip to winter in Hawaii. Not unlike Captain Cook and the Discovery, modern Hawaii winter travelers may also see Montague Island from their jet plane window as they head out across the Pacific for Honolulu.

However, Charlie, a 1947 Stinson model 108-3, would never be considered for transportation to Hawaii. Even with her 14-gallon auxiliary gas tank full to overflowing, she'd barely make it past the 200-mile U.S.-controlled sea space before her motor would cough, sputter, choke, and die. She'd then silently glide to a small splash among the waves, and sink.

But for transportation from Anchorage to Montague Island for three deer hunters, 857 Charlie was ideally suited. She could go there and back and never draw on the 14-gallon auxiliary gas tank unless bad weather required her to detour to Seward, Valdez, or Cordova.

Charlie's pilot learned that there was a small airstrip on Montague Island at McCloud Harbor. The folks who lived there had a small cabin they would rent by the day to deer and bear hunters. They even had a small meat house to stash meat, should the hunters be successful.

And so it was that Lynn Dean and Don Brown, in company with Charlie's pilot, found themselves flying 857 Charlie toward Montague Island on a clear, calm November day. The makeshift windsock at McCloud Harbor was hanging limp when Charlie arrived and Charlie's pilot decided to come in over the sea, land on the end of the strip closest to the water, and taxi to the other end where signs of habitation appeared.

Circling once to check for other traffic, Charlie's pilot entered the downwind leg for landing. Upon turning base, Charlie's pilot observed two people coming out of a house at the far end of the strip. Apparently, the noise of Charlie's engine had alerted the lone residents of Montague Island to their visitors.

The first five minutes of conversation with Montague Island's only locals produced a favorable hunting report, reservations for as long as the three hunters wanted to stay, and an invitation to dinner. Dinner conversation consisted mostly of where to hunt and a warning about Montague's big brown bears.

Almost at first light, the three hunters left their snug, warm cabin and ventured out in Montague's chilly, but comfortable, clear morning. Following directions given by the two locals, the three hunters hiked and climbed to a rock outcropping overlooking a series of open meadows. During the hike, Lynn decided to take up temporary residency on a log where he could observe the meadow from a different angle than from the rocks above.

Don and Charlie's pilot took their position on the rocks just as the first rays of sun broke over the distant peak and warmth and light began filling the little meadow-filled valley. Don's and Charlie's pilot's eyes got heavy with the sun's heat and almost succumbed to the warming rays. Heavy eyelids got quickly lighter when several deer suddenly appeared in the closest meadow. Both bucks and does were immediately present.

Montague had a five-deer limit, but the hunters had decided that due to Charlie's weight requirements, they'd take only two deer each. Don selected two bucks to the right and Charlie's pilot picked out two bucks to the left. At an agreed-upon count, each hunter fired two shots, and two bucks began their journey to the hunters' dinner table.

The confused deer remained in the open meadow. In just a moment, two shots again broke the morning silence as Lynn took his two-deer limit.

The three hunters soon gathered in the meadow to begin the field-dressing process. Lynn was laughing when he came out of the trees. Seems that the morning warmth had overcome his hunter's vigilance and he had dozed off on the warming log. When Don and Charlie's pilot fired their rifles, the noise of the muzzle blast had so startled Lynn that he fell backward off the log. It took him a few moments to gather his wits, find the deer, and take his game.

After cleaning the animals, the three hunters carried one deer apiece on their shoulders and dragged the second one behind them. It was after dark when they returned to camp and hung their meat in the local's meat house. They were tired and thankful that none of the notorious big browns had come to dinner out on the trail.

Next morning they skinned the deer and put them in quarters to fit in Charlie's cockpit. After lunch with the locals, the three hunters gathered themselves and their meat and gear into Charlie and they pointed her nose back to Anchorage. Weather and wind stayed favorable and Charlie was soon parked at her designated spot at Anchorage International Airport.

Twenty years or more have passed since the three hunter friends hunted Montague. Charlie has gone to airplane heaven. Obviously, all the venison has been consumed, Don and the locals at McCloud harbor have left the earth, and Lynn now resides Outside, but returns occasionally.

One thing remains besides the memory of the hunt. Charlie's pilot had his buckskin tanned into a soft leather. His wife fashioned a leather vest that he occasionally wears as the situation arises. Whenever Charlie's pilot wears his Montague Island buckskin vest he remembers the time when he and two friends flew Charlie to Montague Island for deer.

Charlie's Afternoon Moose

There was a recent time when Alaskans went hunting for the pleasure of the hunt and to fill their freezers. It was a time before MacDonald's, the oil boom, and animal activists. Charlie's pilot received his certificate to fly small planes four years prior to the announcement of North Slope oil. It was the time after statehood and before subsistence and sovereignty and wildlife management by New York antihunters and Washington power grabbers. It was the time all outdoorsmen's Alaska fantasies could be realized well within the law and regulation. It was a time when Alaska was for Alaskans and Alaskans were one people.

In those days there were three kinds of hunts: Trophy hunting, sport hunting, and subsistence hunting. Trophy hunting was mostly done by hunters from Outside with money and means to hire a guide. Sport hunting included taking meat for winter stores, but also camping, river and small plane travel, outdoors' camaraderie, smell and feel of a campfire, rain beating on a tight canvas tent, and all the little things that make a hunt more than taking an animal. Subsistence hunting was going to the field from home in car, truck, plane, boat, dogsled, or by any other means, and bringing back the meat.

Lynn Dean didn't have his moose for winter and Charlie's pilot wanted to help. Late in the afternoon toward the last of September, Charlie's pilot and Lynn found themselves flying low back and forth across the Big Susitna River looking for moose grazing or sleeping near a river sandbar big enough for Charlie to land on. They spotted a bull sleeping in a grove of small spruce and birch trees not 100 yards from a long, smooth sandbar. Charlie's pilot flew low over the bar, decided it was safe to land, and performed a picture-perfect short field landing, but kept Charlie's engine running.

A small, shallow branch of the river flowed between the moose and Charlie, making an island of the sandbar landing strip. All Lynn needed to do was wade the small stream, slip through the few trees, and take his moose. Charlie's pilot remained with the plane for a few moments and then took off for a look-around. As Charlie circled the still sleeping moose, Charlie's pilot could not see Lynn until he glanced back at the improvised airport. There stood Lynn signaling Charlie's pilot to return.

Upon landing, Charlie's pilot found Lynn to be wet to his belt, with the explanation that the river was too deep to wade. In the circling and landing, Lynn had become turned around, had gone in the wrong direction, and tried to wade the main river instead of the small stream.

Once he got his proper bearings, Lynn was again a subsistence hunter filling his freezer. Again, Charlie's pilot waited, this time until Lynn waded the shallow water and disappeared into the trees. Then Charlie again took off and circled the unsuspecting moose. Charlie's pilot didn't get a glimpse of Lynn, he only saw the moose's head drop, signaling that Lynn's stalk had been successful and his aim accurate.

After landing, Charlie's pilot gathered his knife and pack and went to assist Lynn with the work part of hunting. By the time the moose was field dressed and one load each packed to the waiting Charlie, it was dark. Too dark to see from one end of the sandbar to the other end.

Charlie's pilot gave Lynn a flashlight from under the airplane's seat, with instructions to walk to one end of the bar and signal his position with the light when Charlie taxied toward him. Charlie's pilot taxied Charlie to the other end of the sandbar.

Under Charlie's seat rested an oily rag used for checking oil levels in Charlie's powerplant. Charlie's pilot removed the rag and drained a small amount of gas from Charlie's wing tanks into the rag. Putting the rag at the end of the bar, Charlie's pilot struck a match and the rag burst into flames.

Quickly, Charlie's pilot taxied toward the waving flashlight beam. Charlie turned 180 degrees at the bar's end and Lynn jumped in. Charlie's engine roared into life. First slowing, then gaining speed, and finally at 60 miles per hour as the little flame from the burning rag seemed to rush toward Charlie. As Charlie came straddle of the fire, Charlie's pilot popped the flaps and Charlie shook herself free from the sand and was airborne and pointing her nose back home with a cargo of half a moose.

Tomorrow Charlie would return and retrieve the balance of the meat.

Charlie's Parachute Experience

The boy scouts of Troop 188 had earned their way to a remote camping adventure on Alaska's Lake Louise. As in all great adventures, much of the adventure was found in the preparation. Not only did the troop prepare the normal things such as getting gear and food together, but they were required to learn outdoor skills, advance in rank, and pass off merit badges.

One of the basic skills all boy scouts must learn is to build a fire in wet weather. Many scouts and leaders call it a one-match fire. The boy is given a knife and one match. He must find dry wood, keep it dry, make tinder, start a small fire, and make it bigger until he can boil a cup of water over the flames.

The scout is taught where to find dry wood under a spruce tree and the paperlike bark of birch. He quickly learns that even in the wettest weather, he will be able to find small dry spruce branches tucked under larger, living, green needle-covered branches further up the tree. His scoutmaster shows him where to gather the branches and how to keep them dry by putting them under his raincoat or in a waterproof bag. He will also demonstrate the merits of building a fire under the tree from which the scout obtained the branches. He explains to the 12-year-old how to clear away dead leaves and branches under the tree, and to build a fire ring to prevent starting a forest fire.

The scout also learns, not only how to build a fire, but the importance of never leaving camp without knowing the fire is completely out. All in all, fire mastery is probably the first skill most scouts learn.

That's the way it started with the boy scouts of Troop 188

as they prepared to camp in the wilderness around Lake Louise. Many of the scouts were on their trail to the coveted Eagle, the highest award a scout can earn. All winter they had passed off camping skills and lifesaving merit badges. By the time summer rolled around they had the skills, and the self-confidence, to venture forth in Alaska's wilderness and come back alive. Mosquito-bitten a bit, and perhaps with a few cuts and bruises, but very much alive, and alive with adventure tales to last a lifetime.

Somehow during one of the training sessions, probably during a time of kidding by the scoutmaster, the scouts had gotten the idea that they were going to have ice cream on one of their remote wilderness days. How the idea grew is a mystery, but is was there as they departed Anchorage.

Charlie's pilot's son was one of the scouts and inquired of the scoutmaster how he proposed to fill his ice cream promise to the scouts.

"Ice cream promise?" the scoutmaster asked. "What ice cream promise?"

Then he learned about the rumor that the scoutmaster was going to show them how to make ice cream in the wilderness. The troop departed Anchorage with the scoutmaster wondering what he was going to do about ice cream on Lake Louise.

Five days into their six-day trip found the scouts 20 miles from the road and anything resembling ice cream. About half-way between lunch and dinner they heard the drone of Charlie's engine and then saw the faded red Stinson circle overhead. Inside Charlie's cockpit sat two fathers of the scouts, one of them being Charlie's pilot.

Before takeoff the two fathers had visited Carrs market's ice cream department and purchased two gallons of ice cream of varied flavors. The half-gallon containers were quickly wrapped in a number of layers of the Anchorage Daily News and then wrapped again with duct tape. The fathers fashioned a makeshift parachute out of a 35-gallon trash bag for each of the four cartons. Eighty-pound fishing line became parachute cords which were tied securely to each of the duct-tape-and-Daily-News-wrapped cartons of ice cream. Parachutes and ice cream were then placed in a picnic cooler and loaded into Charlie's back seat.

Circling Charlie low over the scout camp, Charlie's pilot estimated the wind and plane speed and lined up for a parachute drop. Charlie's passenger forced open the door and dropped and pushed an ice-cream-laden trash bag parachute out on four separate passes over the camp. Then with a wave and a wiggle of Charlie's wings the pair of fathers pointed Charlie's nose back toward Anchorage.

As can be supposed, the scouts had tall tales to tell about their week's wilderness adventures, and at the top of the list was searching the forest around their camp for four-duct-tape-and-Daily-News-wrapped one-half-gallon containers of various flavors of Carrs ice cream. They found all four containers and promptly consumed them.

Perhaps there is a moral in all this. If there is, it's that duct tape works on many things including ice cream parachutes, there is at least one good use for the Anchorage Daily News; and a scout, as the scout law states, is trustworthy. And so is their scoutmaster, even if he promises ice cream in the wilderness.

Charlie's Bear

Morning was well under way when Lynn Dean met Charlie's pilot at Lake Hood Airstrip. Yesterday had been a long, hard day. They'd put in most of a day's work, and then field-dressed and packed out half a moose. Lynn decided to take his rifle with him, saying, "Maybe there'll be a bear on the kill and we'll need an argument to get our moose."

Charlie's engine started on the first crank and the tower cleared Charlie for taxi. At the end of the runway, Charlie's pilot went through a run-up, tested the mags, prop, and control surfaces. "Lake Hood Tower, this is 857 Charlie ready for takeoff."

"Roger, 857 Charlie, hold short. Traffic on final."

"Eight-five-seven Charlie."

In just a moment a red and white Supercub cleared the runway threshold and turned off the runway at the first taxiway.

"Eight-five-seven Charlie. Cleared for takeoff."

"Eight-five-seven Charlie. Straight-out departure requested."

"Straight-out departure approved. Have a nice flight."

Charlie came about into the wind as the prop turned to 3,400 rpm and the old red Stinson picked up speed and jumped into the air. By the time Charlie reached the runway's end, 800 feet of altitude registered on the altimeter and Charlie leveled off for the short hop across Knik Arm.

It wasn't difficult finding the sandbar selected for the day's landing. Prior to landing, Charlie's pilot circled the moose kill just to make sure it hadn't been bothered during the night.

Standing over the gut pile, which it had dragged about 20 feet from where the hunters had left it, a black bear watched

Charlie circle and land. "I'm grateful we brought our rifles," Lynn observed. "Looks like we may need them."

By the time Lynn and Charlie's pilot reached the kill site, the black bear had left. The gut pile had been moved, but the meat was undisturbed. "You watch while I put the meat on the packs. We don't want any surprises by a mad black bear."

Charlie's pilot stood guard while Lynn loaded up the packs. When they were ready, they slipped away down the trail back to the sandbar. It wasn't long before the moose was loaded into Charlie and the hunters were taking off the sandbar airfield.

"Look, the bear's back on the gut pile," Lynn shouted over the roar of Charlie's engine. "I'd like a bear. What do you think? Think I could get him?"

"I don't know, but you can try."

Charlie returned to the sandbar and Lynn gathered up his hunting gear and gun. This time he slipped quietly along the trail looking for his sought-after trophy. Charlie's pilot gave Lynn a few minutes and decided to watch the action from above. Circling over the hunter and quarry Charlie's pilot watched as the hunter and bear played a cat-and-mouse game of hide-and-seek. Finally, the bear tired of the game, and decided to make a move. He crouched behind a log until Lynn had walked past. With Lynn's back to the bear, the bear came over the log and charged the hunter.

Lynn turned at just the right moment, brought his rifle up and fired. The bear went down and Lynn had his trophy. Lynn was still shaking when Charlie's pilot arrived to help dress out the bear. A charging bear leaves an awesome impression. Just ask Lynn Dean.

Charlie's Denali Moose

Ted Pyrah has a heart big as the Matanuska Valley in which he resides. His big heart caused him to agree to accompany a lady senior citizen caribou hunter the air taxi operator would not take out alone.

"I don't know whether he's afraid for me or of me," Helen joked as she asked her friend, Ted, if he'd go with her on a drop-off caribou hunt out of Susitna Lodge on the Denali Highway.

A drop-off caribou hunt in those days—back when a hunter could hunt the same day airborne—when Alaska was for Alaskans—was more of a drop-off meat-gathering expedition. The air charter pilot, who generally knew about where the caribou were likely to be, would fly his clients to the area, locate the caribou, land on a ridge top or gravel bar, and the hunters would go after their winter's meat supply. The pilot would leave and return in the evening and fly the hunters and their meat back to the lodge.

This was the trip Helen wanted to make, but the pilot said, "I'm not dropping off no 75-year-old woman on a herd of caribou and leave her out there. Either you get some man to go with you or I won't take you."

And so Ted agreed to escort Helen on her drop-off caribou-hunting trip. Ted had the whole week off work as he'd planned his vacation to be a hunting vacation. He and Charlie's pilot were going after moose. Ted would take one day out of the moose hunt and go with Helen. They agreed to meet at Susitna Lodge on the Denali Highway where Charlie's pilot would bring Ted at 9 a.m. on the day of the hunt.

Charlie's pilot and Ted spotted moose along their route of flight to Susitna Lodge from Anchorage, spent too much time circling and watching, and arrived late. Susitna Lodge's pilot had become impatient and left for another flight, telling Helen, "If your partner gets here I'll take you tomorrow." Helen knew he really didn't want to take her and was relieved with the excuse of Ted's late arrival.

By the time Ted and Charlie's pilot landed at Susitna Lodge, Helen had left in her car. The folks at the lodge said she was heading for Cantwell. Ted and Charlie's pilot took off and followed the Denali Highway and soon spotted Helen's car approaching a long straight stretch of the road. Charlie's pilot checked the wind by watching the dust made by Helen's car and set up Charlie for a landing on the highway in front of Helen's car.

The landing was routine for Charlie's pilot, but an unusual experience for Helen as she saw Charlie come in low over her car and land on the road in front of her.

Charlie's pilot taxied Charlie to a turnout on the side of the road and Ted was just getting out of Charlie when Helen pulled up. After the excuses and explanations were over Ted asked Helen if she'd just as lief get a moose as a caribou as he told her of the moose he and Charlie's pilot had flown over on the way to Denali.

"Would I!" Helen exclaimed. "I'd rather have a moose any day. I never thought it'd be possible."

With that, Helen got in the plane with Charlie's pilot and Ted drove Helen's car to a pull-off near the area where the moose had been seen. Charlie's pilot was soon circling the moose for Helen to see. When she saw the size of the rack on the huge bull she could only say, "Oh, wow, oh, wow!"

Charlie' pilot landed on the road again and it wasn't long before Ted pulled up and Helen and Ted were off seeking Helen's moose. After a time had gone by Charlie's pilot took off and circled the hunters in time to see both of them shoot and the moose go down. Charlie's pilot landed again, took his knife, saw, and packboard and hiked to the downed moose and Helen, the happy hunter.

By late afternoon Helen's moose was in the back of her car and she was heading for Alaska Sausage in Anchorage to have her meat processed. As she drove off tired, Ted offered, "There goes one happy lady. It's her first moose and he was a big one, and I've got sore muscles everywhere."

Charlie's Missed Moose
by Ron Eggleston

The late fall day dawned cold and crisp with more than a hint of winter in the air. The chill didn't bother Charlie though, in fact Charlie's pilot noticed a little more "spring in Charlie's step" as it were, which seemed to translate to a little more eagerness to take to the morning sky.

This flight took place in the 60s, a time when Alaskans could still fly and hunt the same day airborne, back when Alaska was for Alaskans. The trip from Anchorage across Knik Arm had been uneventful except for Charlie's passenger's penchant for trying to see as far as possible in every direction. This trait might just come in handy for spotting moose. While the sheer exhilaration of being one with the sky was excuse enough for the flight, the practical reason was that the freezer needed replenishing.

Soon Charlie's pilot and her would-be hunter found a lake large enough for Charlie to land on they had spotted moose just on the other side of a brushy hill which ringed the lake's perimeter. Swooping down to the surface of the frozen lake, Charlie's pilot felt a sense of satisfaction in landing as Charlie's tires made fresh tracks in six inches of new snow.

Charlie's pilot suggested Charlie's passenger shoulder his rifle and scout out the moose they had seen from the air. Charlie's pilot would stay behind for a few moments as there was something he wanted to check out.

After Charlie's passenger disappeared through the brush and over the hill he could hear Charlie's engine being reved repeatedly, then brought back to idle. The moose in the meantime had apparently moved on to greener pastures so to speak.

Moving back toward the lake Charlie's passenger found Charlie's pilot standing next to the plane apparently deep in thought and staring down the lake's length. The problem he explained to Charlie's passenger was that one of the craft's magnetos had gone flat and Charlie's pilot was not sure he could take off from the snow-covered lake with both of them on board. Darkness would be falling soon and an attempt would have to be made.

Having little choice Charlie's pilot lined up as long and straight a takeoff as was available and soon Charlie's tires escaped from the snowy lake. Both Charlie's pilot and Charlie's passenger heaved a big sigh of relief as they headed safely for home.

The flight back across the Cook Inlet was without incident as was the landing back at Anchorage International Airport. Once back at Charlie's tiedown spot both her magnetos were pulled out and taken to the magneto repair shop. The shop's mechanic soon discovered that not only was one completely dead but the other one just barely alive. Had it decided to fail on takeoff or over Cook Inlet Charlie's flight would have ended much differently. Charlie's pilot and Charlie's passenger agreed the missed moose could wait for another day. The important part of this whole misadventure was, it ended safely on the ground back at Charlie's parking place..

Charlie's Four-Moose Day

Charlie's pilot guided the 1947 Stinson from frozen lake to frozen lake at about 800-foot altitude. It was late November, weather was clear—crystal clear—but it was cold—almost bitter cold. The plane's tiny cockpit was heated, but not enough to be entirely comfortable without those inside wearing coats, gloves, hats, and warm boots. Besides Charlie's pilot there were two other occupants, each with a hunting rifle.

Neither of Charlie's passengers would be considered a sportsman, at least not by today's standards. This flight took place back in a time when Alaska was for Alaskans, when the moose population across Cook Inlet was used as many Anchorage area residents' winter meat supply. That's why Charlie was flying on this cold, clear November morning, to provide transportation to the outdoor grocery store and back to Anchorage.

N 857 Charlie, model 108-3 Stinson was wearing skis so she could set down on any lake or smooth swamp convenient to where a likely moose could be seen browsing willows. Charlie's pilot would land the airplane as close to the moose as possible, the meat gatherers would exit with their rifles, and slay the moose, one per passenger.

And so it was. Two moose were spotted walking across one of the area's largest lakes. Their direction of travel was noted in relation to the prevailing blowing breeze and Charlie's pilot lined up her landing accordingly. Charlie slipped to a quiet landing some 100 yards slightly behind the moose. Neither moose showed any sign of running off as the freezer fillers removed themselves from Charlie. In fact, they both turned broadside, presenting the perfect shot opportunity as if they had been appointed for this very purpose.

Two shots echoed across the frozen lake and two moose began the final filling of their creation. Charlie's pilot left the subsistence gatherers to their task with a promise to return later in the day. Thirty-five minutes later found Charlie parked at her Lake Hood berth loading up with two new passengers, a young man and his dad, also on a meat-gathering excursion.

Again Charlie circled from frozen lake to frozen lake until two more moose were located near the end of an open, flat, but small, snow-covered swamp. These two moose acted as their peers had done earlier for Charlie's other two passengers. They stood and allowed the boy and his dad to complete their search for winter's meat.

Charlie's pilot left the two to dress out their meat with instructions to pack the moose to a large lake off the end of the swamp. The swamp, long enough for a smooth and safe landing, would not allow for takeoff with a load of meat.

For the next several hours, Charlie made numerous trips from the two lakes where the four subsistence hunters had prepared their game for transport to Anchorage. Darkness had set in before the final load of meat and hunter was transferred to Lake Hood, but it had been a successful day of gathering provisions. Charlie had earned her keep. Four moose in one day.

Charlie's Subsistence Moose

Charlie had successfully carried her four subsistence hunters to a proper conclusion. Each had taken a moose, dressed it out, and cut it up in pieces small enough to be carried in Charlie's cockpit. The morning's two hunters finished their field dressing and Charlie ferried them to the small, snow-covered swamp to assist Charlie's afternoon hunters in packing their winter's moose meat from the swamp to a small, but adequate-sized lake runway.

Charlie's pilot left the four hunters to their work and loaded Charlie with moose meat from the morning hunters' kill. He guided Charlie back to Lake Hood where the morning hunters' family met the airplane and accepted the moose. Several more trips were taken in like manner until the first two moose were in Anchorage and on their way to the happy family's freezer.

Now that the first two moose were taken care of, Charlie's pilot turned to the last two. It was late afternoon and the November sun was just above the horizon when Charlie started back to Anchorage with a load of meat and one of the hunters. Two more trips from the lake in the woods to Lake Hood in Anchorage and all but one of the hunters and an oversized load of moose remained in the field.

As Charlie's pilot left the lake on his last trip he gave the remaining hunter a flashlight and asked him to stand in the middle of the lake when he heard Charlie return. "Wave the light and I'll know what lake you're on and I can find you and I can judge where to set Charlie down."

Afternoon clouds had moved in by the time Charlie returned to the lake and darkness had set in. Alaska's winter nights seldom get pitch-black dark because of light reflected off of snow, so Charlie's pilot was able to locate the moose lake. As Charlie came in over the trees, Charlie's pilot saw the flash of a waving flashlight and set Charlie up for a landing judged by the location of the waving light. As Charlie's skis felt the first touch of snow, pucker brush and hummocks seemed to grow out of what Charlie's pilot thought was the lake.

Charlie bounced from hummock to hummock; willows beat at Charlie's old red paint, and she finally slid to a stop on the lake's ice. Charlie's hunter came running, carrying the waving flashlight. "I didn't mean for you to land here. I waved the light back and forth signaling you not to land. There's an old trapper's cabin over there and I've been visiting with the trapper. I didn't think you'd get back so soon and wasn't able to get out on the lake so I tried to wave you off until I made the lake's center."

Charlie's pilot was filled with quiet anger. The hunter's actions had almost caused a serious accident. Charlie's pilot took his anger out on the remaining moose meat by unkindly loading it into the airplane. By the time the moose was loaded, Charlie's pilot's anger had subsided and he could speak without showing his frustration of nearly killing himself and wrecking Charlie.

"The plane's full, I can't take you on this trip. I'll come back later," Charlie's pilot explained as he tied the meat in with seat belts and fastened his own belt. "If I can't make it back, see if you can stay with the trapper in his cabin and I'll see you tomorrow morning."

With that, Charlie's pilot cranked the starter and Charlie once again motored into action and was soon airborne heading toward Anchorage. As the lights of Anchorage came into view, Charlie's pilot made a decision. He wasn't going back. He'd had enough excitement for one day. His subsistence-hunting buddy would just have to subsist for the night. It'd be a long night for the hunter. But in daylight, Charlie's pilot wouldn't have to rely on a waving light to find the runway. At least that's the line of rationalization Charlie's pilot used to convince himself to leave his buddy overnight in 30-degree-below weather on a frozen lake within 30 minutes of Anchorage. He hoped the trapper was hospitable.

Charlie's Fifth Moose

Charlie's pilot slept in his own warm bed, but sleep did not come easy. He kept waking up thinking about his subsistence hunter friend spending a cold night on a frozen lake. Charlie's pilot convinced himself that his friend deserved it, and, besides, it was dangerous to go back and pick him up considering low clouds and darkness, and the chance that his subsistence hunter friend might mess up the waving light signal again and Charlie'd end up landing in the pucker brush.

The subsistence hunter's moose was deposited safely with the hunter's family, but he was still on the lake, probably spending the night with the lake's lone resident, a trapper in his cabin. If he didn't stay with the trapper, it would be a cold night indeed—pushing past 40 degrees below zero.

At first light, Charlie's pilot was at Lake Hood with his Rupe Goldberg, twisted stove pipe, blowtorch, airplane engine heater breathing super hot air on Charlie's sleeping bag covered powerplant. Despite the cold, Charlie's engine started on the first turn of the prop after only 20 minutes of the heat-induced sourdough-inspired makeshift heater output.

Charlie's pilot's ten-year-old son strapped himself in the front seat beside his pilot dad. He'd been there before and was not only familiar with flying, but quite comfortable with going off over the white land in Charlie. By the time Charlie's cockpit was heated enough to where the 40-below bite was lessened, Charlie was circling the lake where the pilot hoped the subsistence hunter was warm and alive. As Charlie came in low over the cabin, Charlie's pilot could see smoke com-

ing from the cabin's chimney and two men standing out front—
one of them his subsistence hunter friend.

As Charlie turned downwind for landing, Charlie's pilot spotted a huge bull moose standing on the edge of a small lake separated from the trapper's lake by a row of black swamp spruce. In about as long as it took to push in the carb heat control, Charlie's pilot decided on another go-around and lined up for a landing on the opposite side of the moose-occupied lake. Charlie's pilot's freezer was empty. Perhaps father and son could take the big bull and fill their freezer.

Charlie settled comfortably into the soft snow covering the frozen lake and slid to a stop. Even before Charlie stopped, her pilot had his rifle in hand and was standing on the still moving skis while holding back on Charlie's yoke with his other hand. The big bull watched, and made no attempt to flee, but remained standing broadside.

Charlie's vertical stabilizer made a perfect rest for the creation of Johnathan Browning and one shot was all it took to dispatch the bull. Charlie's pilot taxied her to the side of the dead moose and the task of field dressing proceeded.

It was cold, but the warm moose made the job not unpleasant as the field dressing continued. All of the entrails were removed from the carcass when Charlie's pilot's son told his dad that his feet were cold. His dad burrowed a hole between the pile of moose insides and stood his son in the pile. Before long his feet were warmed and he was back helping his dad.

Finally, the moose was cut into small pieces and placed in Charlie's cockpit—big, heavy pieces on the front floor and seat, smaller pieces in back with Charlie's pilot's son sitting on top of his future dinner.

Charlie took off from the moose lake, cleared the row of black swamp spruce, and landed on the trapper lake in one power-on-power-off motion. The subsistence hunter was collected from his new trapper friend, glad to be heading back home to explain his Alaska wilderness winter adventure to his family.

Charlie's pilot would write in his log book—Charlie's fifth moose.

Charlie's Missing Moose

Gravel sprayed off the big tires of 857 Charlie and peppered her horizontal stabilizer. Her aeronautical designers back in 1947 never envisioned her landing on a gravel bar off the Big Susitna River in Alaska. She was made to fly from airport to airport in the South-48, but with the addition of bigger tires on her landing gear and thirty more horses under her cowl, she was called a poor man's 180. A Cessna 180, of course, is every pilot's dream flying machine.

One look at Charlie's horizontal stabilizer immediately gave evidence that this was not her first off-airport landing. The leading edge was pitted where bigger rocks than pebbles had bounced against the aluminum. Most of the red paint was chipped away, exposing the bright color of metal underneath.

Charlie's pilot eased her to a stop, keeping her nose pointed into the wind. Her occupants, the pilot's two teenage children, removed themselves from their seats and stumbled-like to the ground—there is no graceful way to exit a light plane. All three reached back and produced hunting rifles leaning against the back seat.

The object of this exercise was a huge bull moose grazing on a small slough just off the river about a ten-minute walk from where Charlie came to rest near the end of her sandbar airport. It was legal to hunt the same day airborne and Charlie's pilot's family was looking for their winter's supply of meat. They put skinning knives, a small saw, fresh homemade oatmeal-and-raisin cookies and other odds and ends thought necessary to go after a moose.

The short walk through the woods was made in silence;

only the squawk of a lone raven could be heard. The hunting party of three's sense of direction was working and they exited the forest at the exact spot they wanted. Creeping slowly, the hunters took their time to get where they thought they would be able to see the moose and complete their freezer-filling activity by allowing the creation of Weatherby to fulfill the measure of its creation.

To this point in the hunt, everything had gone as planned—or perhaps even better than planned. Everything except that their future steaks and roasts had disappeared—gone. Charlie's pilot and kids stood silently for many minutes, looking deep into the surrounding woods for a glimpse of something brown, hairy, and wearing antlers, but nothing interesting moved or showed itself. Finally they gave each other that knowing look signaling, "Let's go back to Charlie, our moose has got away."

Back at the gravel bar Charlie's pilot walked around the little red airplane looking for anything out of order. Keeping to his habit, he stood on Charlie's oversized tires, removed the gas tank cap and stuck his finger deep enough to feel fuel, confirming what he already knew: Charlie had plenty of gas to let them look around some more and still get safely back home. After draining gas, clearing any water from the fuel line, Charlie's pilot and crew climbed back in and fastened their seat belts for takeoff.

Charlie cleared the gravel bar with ease and was soon circling back over the empty moose slough. To Charlie's pilot's surprise the moose slough was occupied by a big bull moose. The same one as before, in the same spot, and eating the same browse.

Almost without thinking, Charlie's pilot circled back to the gravel bar and repeated the earlier landing. Not a word was spoken. Each hunter knew that being quiet was vital if they were to fill their freezer with this woods-wise moose.

As before, when the wannabe hunters arrived at the moose slough, it was empty, and it stayed empty until they left. By the time Charlie was airborne again, the moose was back to dinner at the slough. Twice more Charlie landed on the gravel bar and her pilot and kids wandered back to the slough in search of their-hoped for meat. Each time with the same results—an empty slough. The moose was gone.

Before the last gravel bar takeoff, Charlie's pilot poked his finger deep into her tanks but couldn't reach fuel. He used a stick to measure remaining gas and mentally computed the time, distance, and fuel requirements to get back home. Eyeing the setting sun and computing gas consumption, Charlie's pilot decided that this day's hunt was over. The next takeoff from the gravel would be this day's last takeoff.

As Charlie cleared the ground and turned toward Anchorage, a big bull moose wandered out of the trees and took a big drink from the slough before going back to eating along the slough's edge. His antlers, free of velvet, reflected in the setting sun as Charlie powered her occupants home. Home to their empty freezer.

Charlie's Ghost Moose

Ted" said Charlie's pilot, as Charlie pointed her faded red nose north, "I know a place where an old, woods-wise moose hangs out. Let's motor over there and take a look." Ted and Charlie's pilot were on their way to rendezvous with one of Ted's friends for a fly-out caribou hunt out of Susitna Lodge along the Denali Highway.

Circling the slough off the Susitna River, as Charlie had done many times with Charlie's Pilot's children aboard, brought the small open spot next to the slough into view. There, standing in the open, was the anticipated moose. He was feeding on willows and watching the 1948 Stinson circle at a safe distance. The Stinson presented no immediate threat and the old monarch kept feeding without looking up again.

"Too bad we don't have more time and we'd give him a go," said Charlie's pilot.

"Let's take the time," Ted exclaimed, his heart rate increasing as he watched the huge moose under Charlie's right wing tip. "My caribou hunt can wait. This moose would fill my whole freezer, if we could get him."

"Ted," Charlie's pilot explained, "I think this is a ghost moose. I've been down on him many times, but he always gives me the slip. By the time I get there, he's gone. By the time I get back to the plane, he's back feeding. And, probably laughing at me. I don't know whether it's worth delaying your caribou hunt or not."

"I'd like to try for your ghost moose. The caribou can wait," Ted said with determination and excitement.

"Okay," said Charlie's pilot, "but we'll have to take it slow and quiet."

Hunting the same day airborne was legal in those days, back when Alaska was for Alaskans. Gas was cheap, old Stinsons like Charlie were affordable, and moose were more plentiful, back when they were managed for the use of man, and before New York and Washington D.C. interests forced weak-kneed Alaska governors to manage moose for wolves.

Upon landing, Ted and Charlie's pilot quietly closed Charlie's doors against the swarm of bugs brought out by the smell of a warm meal in the presence of Ted and Charlie's pilot. Amply applying a dose of Off, the two hunters slipped into the woods and quietly made their way to the slough and the ghost moose. Having been to the slough many times, Charlie's pilot knew the way and they soon arrived at the slough, just opposite of where the old moose had been feeding earlier. Yes, feeding earlier. Now, as with every time in the past, the ghost moose was gone.

"I don't understand it," Ted exclaimed. "Where'd he go? I don't understand it. He's got to be here somewhere."

"I understand it," said Charlie's pilot, "He's a ghost."

"There are no ghost moose," Ted said, "just smart ones."

"I know," Charlie's pilot agreed. "I just wonder where he goes. By the time we get back to Charlie, the ghost moose will be out here feeding again."

Ted and Charlie's pilot leaned against a couple of small birches and thought about the disappearing moose. Maybe 15 minutes went by, without either saying anything or making a sound, both hunters lost in their thoughts about the ghost moose. Charlie's pilot was just about to say, "Let's get back to the plane and on to your caribou hunt," when the ghost moose stood up. Earlier, upon hearing, smelling, or sensing Ted's and Charlie's Pilot's approach, the old, wilderness-wise moose had slipped a few feet into a patch of alders and lain down.

It's not known if he ever saw the hunters, because just as his antlers cleared the alder tops, Ted raised his rifle. His sights and the moose's head topped the alder patch at the same time and both Ted's rifle and the old moose satisfied their existence with the pulling of the trigger.

It took a few minutes for Ted and Charlie's pilot to walk around the swamp and confirm that the moose was dead.

Working as fast as they could, it still took the two happy hunters a couple of hours to field-dress the moose and return to Charlie. Using a hunter's block and tackle tied to a spruce tree, they were able to raise much of the moose off the ground to properly cool it down.

"Well," smiled Ted, "I guess your ghost moose is a real ghost now, probably out there somewhere haunting the happy hunting grounds. Let's go caribou hunting. We'll come back tomorrow and get the moose meat."

Charlie's Prince or Pauper

Fishing Southwest Alaska is the ultimate.

Charlie's pilot made a trip to Southwest Alaska in the old 1948 Stinson Voyager, 857 Charlie. Charlie's pilot's daughter, her friend, and her friend's father completed the party. They flew through scenic Lake Clark Pass and landed at Iliamna. The girls sat in Charlie's swing-back seat, aged with forty years of use. The air through the pass was surprisingly smooth, CAVU weather was wonderful—clear and visibility unlimited. On arrival at the Iliamna airport Charlie entered her downwind leg of the landing approach so that as she dropped her left wing and turned to base her passengers could view their intended Newhalen River fishing site. They could see no other anglers present and they'd have the hole to themselves. Charlie easily landed on the north-south runway, slowing to turn left onto the east-west dirt runway where Charlie parked and was tied down off the edge of the dirt runway between two clumps of brush.

After departing Charlie, their fishing gear loaded in packs, the two fathers and two daughters took the 45-minute hike to Newhalen River, leaving Charlie tethered by the runway awaiting their return. The river was choked with red salmon. They were stacked like cordwood. It was impossible to bring in a line without a fish on. If they had a hookup and it got off, another took its place. They soon had their limit of six salmon apiece, filleted and packed in packs ready for the hike back to Charlie. The balance of the day was spent in catch-and-release fishing off the rocks for resident fish: rainbow, Dollies, and grayling.

As Charlie's pilot recently fished the Newhalen a flood of pleasant memories flowed across his mind. He remembered his teenage daughter and the fun they had together fishing off the rocks and filleting salmon. Now, 30 years later, Charlie's Pilot's daughter has her own family and fishes and recreates with her husband, daughter, and sons. She also remembers the ride in Charlie through Lake Clark Pass and fishing off the rocks with her dad on the Newhalen River.

On Charlie's Pilot's most recent Newhalen outing he didn't get there in Charlie the red Stinson, but came in ERA's twin-engine, radar-equipped, instrument-rated, sleek new flying machine. He didn't walk to the river, he went there in a twin-engine, wide-bodied jet boat and fished areas denied father and daughter on their former venture to the Newhalen. There were no daughters on this trip, just Charlie's pilot and captains of industry. Captains who had paid thousands of dollars for their Newhalen fishing experience.

Charlie's pilot was outclassed by his companions with their Ross reels, Cabala's latest outdoor clothing, and gear he'd only read about in the big three outdoor magazines. The equalizer, and his reason for being with the big boys on the Newhalen was his Alaska experience.

Of course they caught their fair share of fish, kept some for lunch and dinner, captured some on film, and released most of them like father and daughter did on the earlier trip to this fishing paradise.

Compared to Charlie's Pilot's earlier trip to Iliamna with his daughter, this was luxury. Nothing was spared. But, comparing memories—walking to the river and fishing off the rocks with his daughter, and to the latest week's angling adventures—prince or pauper expeditions—if he could do either one again, he'd help his daughter into Charlie, fire up Charlie's engine, fly to Iliamna, hike to Newhalen, and fish off the rocks with his daughter.

Charlie's Last Freedom Flight

Charlie's pilot's son Jesse's first sheep hunt took place on Mt. Gordon among other snow-capped peaks of the Wrangells. It was in the days before the National Park Service entered the scene and stopped hunters from hunting and flyers from landing. It was during the time when Alaska was for Alaskans, when wilderness meant something entirely different than the definition and restrictions given and forced upon us by those in Washington and regulated by the superintendent of the Wrangell-St. Elias National Park. Those were the days never to be forgotten. Days when Alaskans were in charge of Alaska, when government regulation was an invitation to enjoy the freedom of flight, fishing, and the farness of the real Alaska. Then came the "keep out" regulations and restrictions forced upon us by Big Brother and his park ranger bullies.

Charlie, a post-World War II Stinson model 108-3 flew from her tiedown at Anchorage International Airport to the hunting area across from Gold Hill. Circling low and carefully looking over the surface of Nebesna Glacier and finding a long flat area free of holes and cracks in the ice, Charlie's pilot pointed the plane's nose into the wind and landed uphill on the glacier's back. Short field procedures were executed: flaps were quickly brought up on touchdown and brakes were applied hard, bringing the 1948 vintage airplane to a safe stop. Charlie's pilot taxied Charlie to where they intended to tie her down and leave her while they went chasing sheep around Mt. Gordon.

Charlie's pilot used 18-inch mountaineering ice screws for anchors to hold the bird on the glacier in the event wind decided it didn't like 857C parked on top of Nebesna. The hunters spent the first night in a tent on a glacial moraine sand hill off the side of Nebesna. Along about morning the wind decided to test the ice screw anchors and tiedown ropes as well as the tent's wind-shedding ability. Tent, ice screws, and tiedown ropes passed the test and beat the wind. Before they left the glacier for the Dalls' bedroom, they gave the ice screws another couple of turns into the million-year-old ice and checked all tiedown knots.

For the next five days Charlie's pilot and his sons roamed around Mt. Gordon, camping in a different spot each night. As in all sheep hunts Charlie's pilot had been on the hunters had their share of rain, snow, and blow. Toward the end of the week Jesse's creation of Johnathan Browning filled the measure of its creation as Jesse joined the ranks of the few who have taken a pure white sheep at the top of the world.

As the hunters began their downhill climb to their winged transportation back to civilization they could see the red and white Stinson parked on the spine of Nebesna Glacier far below. The mammoth size of Nebesna dwarfed the little flying machine resting on the river of ice where they had left it days before. They descended the mountain and the plane's size seemed to grow as they lost the perspective of hugeness of Nebesna. When they reached the airplane they discovered the ice screws lying on top of the ice and the tiedown ropes listing limply under the wings.

They had not counted on the glacier melting as fast as it did—more than 18 inches in just six days. Had the wicked wind returned before they did the flying machine would have been nothing but a pile of twisted aluminum and airplane fabric in one of the crevasses down the glacier. As it was, a kind breeze began to blow from down below giving them the advantage of a downhill-into-the-wind takeoff. Clearing the glacier, Charlie climbed to altitude and in minutes traced the route the hunter had taken days to walk and climb.

Little did they know as they flew under the tops of Wrangell and Sanford that this would be Charlie's last freedom flight in this area of Alaska's wilderness. With the passing of hunting and flying as they knew it, they also suffered the loss of even their individuality. Where once they were one against the elements, they are now grouped with the masses, restricted to a TV-like experience with the wilderness, while the National Park Service holds the land in trust, for who knows what, except the continuation of the regulators. They have lost the freedom to the real Alaska which is only a memory in the minds of those who were here when the land beckoned, and free men could answer and take their sons to the tops of the mountains to stalk sheep.

Charlie's Last Flight

Eight-five-seven Charlie was a 1948 Stinson model 108-3. She was born red. In the last year of her life she changed her dress and she became metallic blue, with a white stripe running the full length of her somewhat pudgy fuselage. Before becoming blue, she looked her age—one year older than her retired cousin sleeping at the Anchorage Transportation Museum. Before Charlie changed her color, she looked like her cousin's twin. Stinson loved red in the late 40s and most I've seen flew out of the factory with a new coat of red paint. Over time, parked at airports without shade and flying into the sun, Charlie's red faded into an oxidized maroon. But then one day, Charlie's faded, oxidized red color was covered with a blue-colored coat borrowed from General Motors, which they called Cadillac Blue—an appropriate name for the Cadillac of the 1940s' light airplanes.

Winter descended on Alaska's fall hunting season and 857 Charlie started wearing 7-foot long skis instead of the oversized tires she usually sported. The skis were made of wood and the natural, weathered, sawed-lumber look was not complementary to Charlie's new, bright color. The skis fit with the oxidized red, but the new blue with white trim made Charlie look like a lady aristocrat in an evening gown wearing old hiking boots.

As she had done many times in the past, Charlie lifted off Anchorage International Airport and pointed her nose toward the Talkeetna Mountains. Her two passengers, two novice hunters from the South-48, and her Alaskan pilot were wrapped in warm coats, knowing the limited amount of heat produced by Charlie's heater, and the cold weather they could expect once they left Charlie and went chasing moose around the mountains.

Charlie's first landing of the day was atop a snow-covered ridge. Moose wandered the little valley below the ridge and Charlie's passengers were there to take a moose. It was legal to fly and hunt on the same day airborne in those days, back when Alaska was for Alaskans. With rifles in hand, the wannabe hunters left Charlie and headed for their quarry. Charlie's pilot pointed her nose into the wind and pushed her throttle in all the way. Charlie responded with vigor. Now free of two-thirds of her ground-hugging weight, she was airborne within seconds of receiving the *go* command.

Charlie circled low and settled into the snow, lying lightly on a small frozen lake near the hunter's moose. There had been some bumps on landing and takeoff on the ridge and repeated on landing on the lake. Somewhere, either on the ridge top or on the lake, the spring holding Charlie's tailwheel in place broke, and the wheel flopped loosely, dragging along in the snow.

Charlie's pilot, using a piece of iron wire, the handle of a $3/_8$-inch open-end wrench, and a wrapping of duct tape put the spring pack into place to accommodate one more take-off before permanent repairs could be handled. Usually Charlie's pilot would take off empty from such surroundings before allowing people inside the cabin, but with the crippled tail wheel, the unsuccessful moose hunters with their coats, boots, and guns were stuffed in, and Charlie's engine roared in response to gas vaporing in the carburetor when the pilot pushed the throttle.

Most times, Charlie lunged when the propeller's speed wound to 3,400 RPM, but this time she lounged in the snow just a bit. By the time she was airborne too much of the small lake was behind her, not enough distance separated her from the ground, and tall trees seemed to get taller and grow ski-grabbing branches. First one ski, then another, and Charlie's pilot realized this was Charlie's last flight and the best thing to do was to cut the power, control the crash, sacrifice Charlie's wings to trees, and protect the people-carrying fuselage.

Charlie gave up hard, but in losing her wings, she saved her passengers and she died with dignity. Had she been able to hear, she would have heard her pilot explain the reason he had guided her to such a twisted end —I just ran out of air speed, altitude, and ideas—all at once.

Hiking Alaska

Hiking Alaska

Which trail is the best trail in Alaska to hike? The one you're hiking on, of course! Pick out a trail and gear up!

Hiking Alaska is like hiking an area the size of thirteen states. It's as big as Texas times two. Alaska has the largest National Park in the continent, the highest mountains, the longest rivers, and the largest and smallest national forest. Alaska is a state with cities and towns nestled in prime hiking land and pristine wilderness.

The Greatland beckons hikers to the tortuous Chilkoot Trail, winter wonderland White Mountain playground, sand dune deserts as far north as Nome, and bubbling hot springs above the Arctic Circle. It summons them to the summit of Mt. McKinley and the quarter-mile pack to photograph a mountain sheep, to deep echoing sounds along the islands of the Panhandle, the Greatland beckons people who love to get into the backcountry—hikers!

Alaska hiking trails are accessed by road, boat, train, or plane. Most of them sight glaciers, abundant wildlife, and surprising plant life. Many are not trails at all. They are walks above timberline, out of the brush, and off the beaten path.

Alaska is a place to be alone or meet others on the trail. Alaska—where you can flag down a train and go to another hiking trail or fishing spot. In Alaska, a hiker can spend a day or a week in unspoiled wilderness and be but a few minutes away from the highway or town.

But don't expect to see it all. If you explored a thousand square miles of the Greatland a day, you couldn't see it all in your lifetime.

City of Trails

It has been said that Anchorage is only 30 minutes from Alaska. Alaska is not in the city or along the highway. Alaska, the real Alaska, is only 30 minutes away from these. Alaska is wilderness. It is hiking the wild, fishing in unpolluted water, sighting a bear, tracking a moose, tricking a fish, or as Robert Service put it "standing in some mighty mouthed hallow that's plumb full of hush to the brim, and watching the big husky sun wallow in crimson and gold and grow dim." Anchorage is only 30 minutes away.

Visitors to Anchorage and residents who do not frequent the wilderness remind us of the man who went to a buffet, ate his fill at the hors d'oeuvre table, and told everyone how great the food was. Alaska is not just hors d'oeuvres. It's not even soup and sandwiches. Alaska is a banquet. It's a seven-course meal with dinner music, mood lighting, and a Carnegie Hall all-star cast performance and Anchorage is only 30 minutes away.

Thirty minutes from Anchorage and hikers can see, feel, touch, taste, hear, and smell Alaska. They can get away from the city and onto an uncrowded trail within 30 minutes. They can leave behind the concrete and the artificial and be in wilderness within a half hour of their job or home.

Anchorage, bordering on the Chugach State Park and Chugach National Forest, is a city of trails. Take any road off the Glenn or Seward Highway and it will lead to a trailhead. It would take a hiker at least one summer of constant hiking to trek all of the trails from Portage to Knik. New trails are constantly being developed and old ones upgraded and maintained. Yes, Anchorage is the city of trails. Wilderness Trails, and it's only 30 minutes from Alaska.

Bird Creek Trail

Bird Creek Trail begins in a birch forest and climbs into an alpine area above Turnagain Arm. It is one of the first hikes open to sufferers of cabin fever. Early spring, warm Chinook winds blowing from Prince William Sound over Portage Pass into Turnagain Arm, melts snow and dries the trail along the southern exposed hills. The southern exposure brings early flowers to an area surrounded by snow. Spring hikers often find an open spot exposed to the sun, and attempt to obtain a preseason tan by spreading a space blanket and basking in the season's first rays.

A few years ago, before the trail was clearly marked, we bucked our way to the saddle between Bird and Ship Creeks. It was a fall hike. The trail was dry and free of snow. Arriving at the saddle at midday, we stopped for lunch. As we ate, we imagined we were the area's first visitors. It seemed we had stepped back in time and were discovering Alaska. It was wonderful to survey the valleys and to see sheep on the mountaintops. Perhaps the first men to have done so. We were alone in a time-locked land and the feeling was grand.

As we proceeded over the saddle into Ship Creek Valley, we were immediately brought out of our time warp into the 20th century. There on the hillside were the remains of earlier hikers' lunch. They had packed in Government Issue C rations and had scattered the cans over a large area. We picked up their mess, but our hike had been desecrated. The experience forcibly drove home the need to pack out what is packed in.

As we returned to civilization carrying the remnants of someone else's bad manners, I was reminded of a thought expressed to me ages ago by a teacher long since departed, "You can tell the character of a man by the garbage he leaves behind."

Speechless Brothers

Our wait at the Homer small boat harbor was not unpleasant while we waited for the arrival of our guide, Kevin Sidelinger. Lars and I witnessed boats of all shapes and sizes being backed down the ramp and launched to ports who knows where. Some were sleek manufactured craft. Others homemade. Some big. Some small. Some open. Some enclosed.

One anxious boater forgot to put in the drain plug before launching and nearly sank his craft before getting it back on the trailer to drain, put in the plug, and relaunch. Timed with the relaunch, Kevin's boat slipped to the dock. Greetings and introductions were short and in just a moment, our gear was stowed aboard his "work boat." Kevin explained the safety features, told us where to sit, and we made a wakeless exit from the harbor.

Kevin and his wife Cindy call Halibut Cove home and headquarters for their alpine llama trips. Enroute, Kevin explained that the llamas had been transported from the cove to the lagoon earlier using this same boat. Animals and crew were awaiting our arrival.

Cindy and the balance of our party greeted us as we stepped ashore. Here we met the animals, as Kevin and Cindy affectionately call the llamas. After being introduced to the bearers of our packs, Conan the Barbarian and Boone the Explorer, we were soon on a first-name basis.

Dan and Linda, the leaders of our group, handled the loading with expert ease. Dan explained as he filled the packs with our gear, if the pack is too heavy or unbalanced, the llama will merely lie down. If the pack is loaded correctly, they will carry it for hours without prejudice. In fact, the Indians of South America call the llamas speechless brothers. Only a brother would carry the burdens they do without complaint. Boone and Conan accepted our gear without complaint.

Our destination was an alpine lake at the base of Chocolate Drop Mountain. Chocolate Drop is a small, 4,000-foot-high peak set in the center of a large valley. At the base of Chocolate Drop we made camp.

Twenty yards from our tent was a small, clear-water creek, terminating in the lake. Lars and I unpacked our fly rods before the tent was up. My first cast with a polar shrimp brought a tug to the line. The bow made several small runs, always staying in the current. Finally I maneuvered him out of the fast water. By the time I had him beached, an audience gathered. "Trout for supper," Cindy announced. "Catch three more." The first one had been so easy I readily accepted the challenge.

Supper was late that night as Lars and I labored for the next three hours to accomplish our task. I learned again to never judge a fishing hole on the first cast. Later, Kevin took us out in the canoe where we were able to even the score on the rainbows.

The next morning we assaulted Chocolate Drop. The conversation at the top turned to the animals. We found them to be wonderful companions on the trail. They seemed to anticipate what was required. They are quiet, docile, intelligent, and extremely sure-footed. Because of their padded feet, they are able to travel over a wide variety of terrain and steep mountainsides and trails.

Around the evening fire, enjoying a meal of Cindy's open-pit barbecue spare ribs, our zoology lesson continued. Each animal can carry three or four times what a person can comfortably pack. Because of the animals, we had luxuries on this trip that were uncommon or nonexistent on most backpack trips.

For three days Lars and I enjoyed exploring, canoeing, fishing, and climbing in Kachemak State Park. We got closer as father and son and to the land we call home. And, we wished for more as we bid our speechless brothers goodbye.

It came to our memory, on our return to the Homer small

boat harbor, that the Homer Spit is the end of the Pan American Highway that begins in Argentina. This road passes through Peru, Bolivia, and other South American countries, the ancient home of the llama. I suppose it is only fitting that one of the world's oldest domestic animals be earning its living at the end of the road that began close to the animal's beginning.

Oh, yes, before I forget. Concerning the llamas' reputation for spitting. The only spit we saw was the Homer spit.

Hiking and Wildlife

In the early 1970s there was a renewed interest in placer gold exploration and mining in the Nelchina area and the old trails north of Sheep Mountain were used again. Early users of the Chickaloon-Knik-Nelchina Trail began their trek at Knik on the north shore of Knik Arm of Cook Inlet. Civilization, towns, farms, roads, and highways have replaced or covered the old trail. Hikers now access this historical trail at the Chickaloon Trailhead, other trailheads along the Glenn Highway, or Old Man Creek Trailhead, the trail's most northern access point.

This whole area is crisscrossed with animal and human trails that would fill a book if only a brief description was used for each trail. I've lived in Alaska and walked these trails for more than three decades, and I'm still discovering new paths and places to visit and new ways to get there.

Once while hiking one of the old trails, I met a young couple and asked how they liked the trail. They said they had enjoyed the rich abundance of wildflowers but had hoped to see wildlife. I told them most wildlife bedded down during the day and were out feeding in early morning and late afternoon. I suggested they take a nap and hike the trail again in the early morning or late evening, bring binoculars, stop in open areas, and they would probably see fox, caribou, and moose. When I talked to them next they were hooked on Alaska and her "wildlife everywhere."

One spring, my 15-year-old daughter, Diane, and I spent two days and one night on Sheep Mountain observing and photographing a band of Dall rams. Sheep have excellent eyesight and can pick up the slightest movement if people allow themselves to be seen. Once seen, however, don't move out of sight. As soon as sheep cannot see the person they have been looking at, they will quickly move away. We watched our sheep for an hour or more and they did not move. I told Diane about sheep running if they saw us, then couldn't see us. She decided to test the theory. As soon as she moved out of sight, the four big rams quickly stood up and walked over the hill and out of sight.

Alaska's not "full of wildlife" as some brochures want you to believe, but there's plenty. It's called wildlife because it's wild. Wild animals have habits peculiar to the species and season. If hikers want to add wildlife to the joy of the hike they must know wildlife and hike with the habits of wildlife in mind.

Winter Trail

Winter hikes in the far north demand a different attitude than more conventional hikes elsewhere. Hikers must adapt their mental makeup to cope with darkness and cold that can literally drive a person over the brink.

This is winter wilderness Alaska right out of the pages of Jack London and Robert Service. Winter hikes are not for the unprepared. A minor incident may end in major tragedy. For the prepared and informed a winter hike can lead to high adventure. The three most important rules of winter hiking in Alaska are: (1) be prepared, (2) be prepared, and (3) be prepared.

My experience on the winter trail has given me many unusual memories. Once, at 59 degrees below zero, I had to preheat white gas with a small fire before it would vaporize enough to burn in the Coleman stove and lantern. Cooking breakfast was a problem in subzero weather one morning, when frozen raw eggs had to be peeled before they could be put in the frying pan. Pancakes cooked over an open fire were burned on the outside and nearly raw in the middle. The fire could only give enough heat to cook the batter next to the pan. The outside temperature was so low, it kept the top and middle from enough heat to change the batter to a pancake.

I have seen breath vaporize and freeze on a beard causing whiskers to break when touched. At 60 degrees below, spit turns to ice before it hits the snow, any exposed flesh will freeze within 30 seconds, and extremely cold air entering lungs can cause damage. When ice fishing, fish are immediately flash-frozen when pulled from the hole in the ice.

Unexplained phenomena occur in cold, clear air. Once I saw a large, Chicago-like city, complete with high-rises and skyscrapers. It wasn't a cloud formation but the refracted image of the city projected against the deep-blue southern sky. Another time, standing on level ground at night, I was able to see taxiway lights of an airport more than 35 miles away.

Yes, as Robert Service wrote, "There are strange things done in the midnight sun." For the adventurous and well-prepared, a winter hiker will find, "Arctic trails have their secret tales," and the strangest sights of the northern lights may well be the ones the Greatland reserves for you.

Trent "Lewis and Clark" Clawson

Matanuska River Park Trail system can rightly claim the shortest hiking trail in the largest state in the union. This trail system includes recently constructed paths as short as 45 yards.

Cleared paths begin at four trailheads in the park camping area. A fifth trailhead near the fenced softball complex is the start of another trail. All the trails loop into, or connect with, the trails of the system. This is an ideal group of trails to take youngsters, even toddlers, to give them a beginning appreciation for wilderness. Although the trails are never far from the camping area they give the impression of backcountry, especially to the young and those familiar only with city life, sidewalks, and paved streets. These short trails are good hikes to introduce kids to backpacking, but never let them go on their own unattended. Trails near the icy cold, fast-moving Matanuska River could be dangerous for young, inexperienced hikers.

Following the trails of the system will take hikers along paths leading to and paralleling the Matanuska River. For the young, following a map, furnished free by the park, to areas with exciting names is a never-to-be-forgotten thrill. Names like Long Pond Trail, Duck Pond Trail, Duck Pond Spur, Swan Pond, and River Spur Trail conjure up images in their minds of backcountry and wilderness intrigue.

My 8-year-old grandson, Trent, and I hiked the system on a July afternoon. It was a special thrill for him to talk to the park director and obtain a map and instructions. He listened intently and plotted our course on the map with a pencil. It took less than an hour, under Trent's leadership, to complete the trails he had marked. He carefully guided us from loop to loop and safely past the dangerous Matanuska River. We saw birds, and dog tracks closely resembling those of a big wolf.

From Trent's conversation upon our return to civilization, in his mind, we had accomplished a feat equal to climbing Mt. McKinley. Hearing him explain to his grandmother about all the things we did along the miles of backcountry wilderness trails, I think he thought we had been gone for weeks not minutes. I look forward to being guided again in the wilderness by Trent "Lewis and Clark" Clawson.

The Final Four

The last chapter in our *Hiker's Guide to Alaska* is titled, The Final Four. The Final Four are not for everyone; they are for the few and the brave. They are for the few willing to pay the price, brave hikers of courage accepting the challenge to climb Mt. McKinley, North America's tallest peak, to trudge the Golden Stairs of Chilkoot Pass, to winter-walk the Iditarod's 1,000-mile wilderness, or trek the Dalton Highway's edge from the Yukon to the Arctic. The Final Four require rigorous training, dedicated practice, special equipment, and support services.

Other hikes in the *Hiking Guide to Alaska* can be accomplished by the average person in an afternoon, a day, on a weekend, or in the time frame of a vacation. The Final Four require planning, preparation, training, conditioning, and even some expense. Not many of us are brave enough to challenge the Final Four, but after reading about them I'll wager you'll think about it, you may even write for more information, and a few may give it a try.

The Final Four are for everyone who ever dreamt about looking down on the world from 20,300 feet, whose secret desire is to cross the Yukon River and find the Arctic Circle, or whose fantasy is following the trail of 98.

The Final Four are for the brave few—perhaps you.

Miss Shapen

Miss Shapen One

In the mid-50s, Standard Oil Company discovered oil on the Kenai Peninsula and punched a road allowing access to Swanson River. New Alaskans Frank Ackerman and I built a 12-foot, cartop boat out of plywood, purchased a five-horsepower Evenrude to push the now christened Miss Shapen, and became one of the Swanson's first anglers.

Each Friday evening would find us with Miss Shapen on top of my old Nash Rambler heading for the Kenai Peninsula. We'd arrive at Swanson River about 9 p.m., load up our obnoxious-looking craft with camping and fishing gear and go upriver as far as we could before it got too dark to travel.

Frank and I developed a quick camp setup routine, cutting into only about ten minutes of fishing time. After camp was established, we'd get out the fishing gear, and, in the half-light between sunset and sunrise, we'd catch a couple of Swanson River rainbow for our late dinner. One of us would fix our meal while the other continued catch-and-release fishing. After dinner, we'd retire and set the alarm for an early rising.

Our habit was to get up early Saturday morning, take Miss Shapen, and fish and explore further upriver. We'd see some new country, watch wildlife, catch and release more than a hundred rainbows before noon, and then return to our tent for lunch. We'd break camp and float and fish back to where we'd parked the car. We'd then head for Anchorage, taking turns driving and sleeping and pulling into our driveway around midnight.

Most of our free time during the week was spent in getting ready for our next Miss Shapen-Swanson River outing. This continued until fall. It was one August Friday evening after we'd pitched camp in what had become by this time a familiar spot, that Frank hooked into the fightingest rainbow either of us had ever seen. In the twilight, we could see Frank's fish jump and dive and jump again and again. We had no idea where this monster came from. Swanson River rainbows are plentiful but mostly pan size. This fish was at least 10 times bigger than even the biggest Swanson River rainbow either of us had ever caught.

Frank held on, the gear held out, and the fish finally gave up. Frank eased the fish into a shallow, grassy notch in the river's bank. I grabbed the flashlight so we could see what this super Swanson River rainbow looked like. When the light played on the fish's side we discovered it was no rainbow at all. It was a silver salmon. We hadn't even thought about salmon running in the Swanson. Frank's first silver was only one of many as the weeks worked toward winter.

As silvers increased, rainbow catches declined, but we didn't care, we were living every Alaska fishing fantasy we'd ever had. All summer long we'd had the river to ourselves. We explored, camped, and fished. This was the Alaska each of us had dreamed of: uncluttered, untamed, free of people, and full of fish. And, the creation of our own hands had taken us there—Miss Shapen.

Miss Shapen

Miss Shapen, 12 feet long, constructed of quarter-inch plywood, and covered with two layers of fiberglass, gained her name by an error in her construction. Miss Shapen came into being in 1958 for the sole purpose of taking two new Alaskans to the Kenai Peninsula's newly accessible Swanson River. Miss Shapen was conceived and constructed in one workweek of evenings late in the spring of '58. In the water, she was stable with her 24 inches of freeboard and high bow. The bow is what gave her her name. One of Miss Shapen's gunnels was longer than the other, causing a wow in the bow. She always looked like she was turning to the right, even when turning left. The balance of her lines were fit and perfectly suited for her reason for being.

Frank Ackerman and I, the builders of Miss Shapen, took her to the Kenai each Friday evening and brought her back home Saturday night for most of the summer of her birth. The Swanson River, a newly discovered fishing stream, produced catches of rainbow trout, small in size, but huge in numbers. Frank and I were novice anglers and made the mistake of bragging about our Kenai catches until a couple of our friends began believing us.

Given another opportunity, I wouldn't have told a soul about the Swanson River rainbow. For the first few weeks of summer, Frank and I had the river to ourselves—just us, and the river, and the fishing. Then one Friday evening as we pulled into our customary parking spot on the river's edge we saw another car with an empty canoe rack on top. We were, maybe not devastated, but surely disappointed to think that someone was on our river, catching our fish, and seeing our moose. And then we recognized the car as belonging to one of our friends.

The week before Frank and I had accidentally found a small stream entering the Swanson. The Swanson, in many places, is more swamp than river. At one of these swampy spots a side stream enters at just such an angle that it melts into the river a few yards from where it emerges from a tangled growth of willow—which further hides the stream from a boater. The week before, we'd forced our way through the tangled wall of willows and discovered a picture-perfect trout stream complete with deep pools and riffles holding trillions of hungry rainbow. We thought we'd died and gone to heaven and, to our regret, we were free in telling our friends about our discovery. Now they were in their canoe on our river waiting for us to find them and show them our new, magazine-cover-like rainbow hole.

Seeing our friends' car parked in our spot and knowing they were upriver in their canoe woke Frank and me up. As we went up the river, we resolved that we would never again say anything about the Swanson, the rainbow, or our newly discovered rainbow factory. And further, we'd die before we'd show it to anyone.

As we approached the entrance to our secret hole we could see our friends in their canoe further up the river. We let them get out of sight around a bend and we slipped Miss Shapen into the clear-water, slough-like little stream's tall grass-lined delta. We pulled Miss Shapen as deep into the willows as we could, which perfectly hid our presence from anyone traveling the river and not knowing the little stream was there.

We fished and we fished—we caught and we released, and we heard the putt-putt of our friend's outboard going up and down the river oblivious of us secreted away beyond their searching eyes.

We never again told anyone of our Swanson River successes or the location of our private fish hatchery. We even almost lied when our friends asked where we were as they motored up and down the river, not finding us nor the fish. We let them go away thinking our tales of the previous week's trips were just fish stories. I don't think they ever fished the Swanson again, and, if you've heard about the Swanson River rainbow, I know you didn't hear it from Frank or me.

And don't go running down to the Kenai when the ice goes out. You don't believe there really is such a place, do you, or there ever was a boat named Miss Shapen?

Miss Shapen With the Wow in Her Bow

Miss Shapen, with the wow in her bow, was a good little boat. She wasn't pretty much good for pretty, but she was pretty much good for stout. That's the way she came together. It wasn't planned, it just happened. Being constructed by two novice builders, with no written plans or experience, she came into being to fill a need—sleep upside down in the backyard from midnight Saturday to 5 p.m. Friday, and then ride on top of the old Nash Rambler down the highway to Swanson River. She'd then provide transportation from fishing hole to fishing hole for her builders.

Had Miss Shapen been people instead of a boat, she would have known something was different when she was awakened one Monday evening in late August. There was more than just a nip in the air. There was a kind of excitement.

Once on the river, even though it was nearly dark, Miss Shapen was loaded for the trip to camp and this time her load included food for a week, and rifles along with the customary fishing gear.

Having negotiated the river numerous times over the summer, we felt no fear in heading upriver on this cloudy evening with darkness rapidly slipping toward us. We could tell it had been raining, but for now it was just high clouds, no rain.

Usually we were in a hurry to get upriver and set up camp and get to fishing, but not this trip. We were moose hunting and we knew there would be no hunting until daylight the following morning, so we just puttered along.

About the time we started up the river we could see a full moon trying to force its light through the high-thinning clouds.

When we reached the first set of rocks, the clouds all but disappeared around the moon and moonlight quickly brightened the area we were traveling.

Just above the first set of rocks is the only long, narrow stretch of water on the Swanson. It was here that the aurora joined the celestial light show. Frank, sitting on the wow in the bow, brought out his harmonica and began playing familiar tunes, mostly old-style hymns.

We putted along with the glory of the moon, stars, and northern lights, accompanied by Frank's music, keeping us deep in thought. As the river widened, our field of vision expanded. On up the river a ways we caught the reflection of a foreign shape. As we came closer the shape materialized into two couples standing in a boat better than twice the size of Miss Shapen. The motor was tilted up.

As we approached the boat and turned off our quiet little 5-horsepower Evenrude, we saw four very wet, cold folks standing in a disabled boat. Seems like it had rained all day. Their boat, too big for the Swanson, and their motor, reaching too deep in the water, had suffered one more bout with a rock than they had shear pins. They were too wet and scared to go downriver and they were far from a good camping area.

We tied a rope to their bow and towed them to a good place to camp. As we were leaving, now loaded up with thank-you homemade cookies, one of the women spoke up with this parting thought, "We were feeling pretty good when the moon came up, the stars came out, and the northern lights began to play. But when we heard your harmonica music we thought you were angels sent to rescue us." We didn't argue. We just took the cookies and went on our way. And nobody laughed at Miss Shapen with the wow in her bow.

Fishing Alaska

What's a Fish Worth

What's a fish worth? One fish. Not a boat load, not a stringer of lunkers, not even a trophy. Just one fish. One little fish. What's one little fish worth? I'm not asking about a king salmon or a rainbow trout. My inquiry is concerning a Dolly. What's one Dolly Varden char worth?

One spring, Easten and I got the desire to go fishing. We knew we were pushing the season a bit, but we just couldn't wait to get out. A call to Craig Ketchum, and a day later we were at one of Ketchum's Kenai Lakes cabins.

We had fishing on our minds and even before gear was put in the cabin, we had the boat motor installed and were heading for the spot Craig had advised. Two loons crossed our intended route to the fish, and we slowed to let them pass. Alternately, one would dive, apparently searching for food, and the other stood guard. We forgot fishing for the moment, and stopped to watch and listen. As we watched the loons, we became aware of spring's first green appearing on the bushes and trees along the shore, and realized it was the beginning of summer. After a time we started the outboard and moved on, leaving that part of the lake to the loons.

Craig advised us to troll the edges of one of the lake's islands. As we throttled down, a movement on shore attracted our gaze. There she stood. A huge cow moose, staring at us from the protection of a small swamp spruce. We stopped, killed the engine, drifted with the afternoon breeze, and watched. Deciding we presented no threat, she moved toward the lakeshore. Trying to follow, almost walking between her back legs, was a newborn calf. We were perhaps witnessing his first steps. The breeze gently, slowly pushed us away from mama moose and we watched as she disappeared with her offspring into the cover of spruce, birch, and brush.

Our earlier near panic of getting to the fishing slowed by loons and moose, now moved to a pace almost matching the speed of the greening of the trees. For some reason, it seemed better to just move slowly, and see what other pleasant surprises our fly-in lake held. Before we reached Craig's selected spot, we saw two more loons; a flock of geese were V-ing north, groups of ducks made low passes overhead and moved on. A pair of mergansers worked the lakeshore. Small birds called out their warning and greeting.

A couple of hours passed before we set up our rods. We took our time. Tied the swivels on with knots like we were pros. Easten captained the boat and I set out our lines. One on each side over the gunnels. I handed Easten his rod and he was soon playing pull and tug with a little fish. A little Dolly, about 12 or 14 inches.

We'd missed lunch, stopping to buy licenses, and hurrying to meet Craig's takeoff time. Evening arrived with the landing of the Dolly, and being hungry, we decided to use the season's firstfruits for supper.

Easten cleaned his catch and we wrapped it in strips of bacon and fried it between slices of potatoes. Other foods were added and dinner was served. The best fish we'd ever eaten.

Next morning we took out the .22 rifle and killed four soda pop cans with two boxes of bullets. It took about three hours for the bullets to disappear and the cans to succumb. We motored around the lake and became better acquainted with its resident mama moose and her calf, the loons, and mergansers. We forgot to fish. And then Craig came to pick us up.

Since that day, Easten and I rarely have a fish dinner, or even talk about fishing, that the conversation doesn't end up at the Dolly dinner wrapped in strips of bacon, served with fried potatoes, and eaten at twilight in Ketchum's Kenai cabin.

What's a little Dolly worth? I know one that's worth plenty, gets more precious every day, and will increase in value after I'm gone and Easten tells his children, my grandchildren, about the spring he fished with his Dad on Alaska's Kenai Peninsula, and the Dolly who came to dinner.

For Kids Only

This is for kids only. If you want to go fishing more next summer begin planning right now. Maybe you could ask for a fishing rod and reel for your birthday. Best yet, save your money and give your dad or mom fishing equipment for their birthdays. Don't just quit at birthdays. Remember parents have anniversaries: a good time to give a few flies or a new Daredevle or two. Have your own "kids take parents fishing" day, and do something special for them. Take out the garbage or sweep the walks without being asked. If you remember them now, they'll remember you when fishing season rolls around.

Remind your folks that you will be a year older this year, more mature; and let them know you will not cry with cold feet. Show them you will take better care of the fishing gear next season by taking better care of your things now. Offer to clean out the tackle box and oil the reels. Keep your bedroom clean.

Call around or write and get brochures and information on different trips you think they would like to go on. Determine the price. Find out which guides and what services will accept kids. See if they have special rates for you. Encourage making reservations early. Try to earn money to help pay your share.

Let other interested adults know you like to fish. Write a letter to grandparents telling of your interest in fishing. Send them a subscription to Alaska Outdoors® magazine. Talk to neighbors who fish. Do something nice for them. Find out when National Fishing week is. Ask your parents, grandparents, and neighbors, and find out who took them fishing when they were young. Get them to talk about their fishing experiences when they were growing up. Let them know how important it is to take a kid fishing.

Try these things, because if you don't get to go fishing this year as much as you want, it's your fault.

Vibes

by Carrie Smith

I've heard it said that one must have a vibe in order to catch fish in Alaska. This is a special signal the angler sends to the fish through the rod, and the fish is mystically drawn to the hook. Some call it vibes, some say it's skill, and others just call it plain luck. Whatever you call it, I know I don't have it.

I've been on fishing trips where every person around me was reeling in fish, and I'm sitting there wondering if the guide actually missed putting a hook on the end of my line. Did he just forget about me? Is this some weird initiation joke all guides play on the rookie? Maybe he's a chauvinist and can't take the chance I might outfish him?

I've fished the Kenai, Kachemak Bay, English Bay, Lower Cook Inlet, Upper Russian, Susitna, Lake Louise, Talkeetna, Talachulitna, on fly-outs aplenty, and various points in between. I'm not saying I haven't EVER caught a fish. I have. But comparing the number of times I've been out and the number of those slimy creatures I've actually got into the boat or the shore is, well … embarrassing!

There was the 35-pound king from the Kenai, the Homer halibut the guide lost when the gaff slipped (a likely story), and the burbot caught in Lake Louise last year. Did I mention you can't keep burbot caught in Lake Louise? I did catch an English Bay Dolly when I was eight years old. My dad hadn't got to the reeling-in lesson yet, so when this little thing hooked on, I threw the rod over my shoulder and ran like a maniac up the beach. The poor fish didn't stand a chance. It bounced on the top of the water like a well-thrown skipping rock and I'm sure it died of shock before my dad unhooked it. I have the picture to show my kids. "See, mom actually has caught a fish." My 7-year-old just rolls her eyes and walks away.

My husband says you have to keep at it and I give up too soon. But over the years I've come to accept the lack of vibes in my fishing life and I just kick back in the boat and work on my tan. There are other things about fishing trips I've learned to enjoy.

The trip to Lake Louise is my favorite: the quaintness of Sutton, the slate-gray beauty of the Matanuska River, and the cobalt blue of the glacier. The kids are asleep about the time we drive through the valleys before Eureka and I tell my husband, AGAIN, how great it would be if we could move out there with the kids and actually make a living in those green, wild valleys.

The best part about the trip and all the drives I take with the family is watching them play in Alaska's outdoors. Their blue eyes shine brighter and their cheeks are a couple of shades rosier. My husband is a little more handsome (is that possible?) while driving the boat. The pictures we take seem to turn out more vivid and we sleep a little better at night. Must be all that fresh air. I might miss these things if I was preoccupied with catching fish.

As Robert Service wrote, "It isn't the gold that I'm wanting so much as just finding the gold." There are thousands of people who can only dream of living in the Greatland. Some of those people spend thousands of dollars each year to get just a taste of our everyday lives. What a shame if we only appreciated it when a fish was dangling on the end of our fishing line. It sounds like a sour-grape-non-vibes rationalization, but if all I wanted was fish, I could go to the seafood counter at Carrs. Besides, I never heard anyone say going to the supermarket was the best part about getting his fish.

Two Records

Two records were at stake. One to break, one to preserve.

Andy thought Lars's record of never being skunked on a fishing trip showed he hadn't ever fished the shoulder season, but only fished at the height of the runs. Whatever the case, Lars Swensen was going to do his best to protect the guide's integrity and preserve his self-proclaimed record of never coming home without catching a fish.

Andy Couch, FishTale River Guides guide, was pushing the shoulder season to the limit. Last year he'd predicted an early run and been successful in guiding his clients to the first king of the season on the Little Susitna River on May 17. This year he hoped to duplicate the event one day earlier, May 16.

And so the stage was set. The Little Susitna River played host to these two record breakers' informal, but important, world records. Fish gods won't let anglers catch important fish early in the day. After 10 hours of hard, but unrewarded, fishing, Andy announced, "Only two more holes."

Two more holes and defeat. But the fish gods were kind, and a sea-bright, fresh king salmon took the bait. A ten-minute intense battle ended with the season's first catch being held high for photographs between two happy, lucky anglers.

Andy Couch, FishTale River Guide, had extended his season one more day. The envelope was pushed to May 16 for the first Little Susitna River king.

Lars Swensen again went home with fish, never yet skunked on a fishing trip.

Two records—one broken, one preserved. Two happy anglers.

Top Ten Rivers

I'm often asked where I think the best place to fish is. If my first quick response of "Whatever river you're standing on," is pressed further, I'll usually come up with a list of the ten most popular rivers. My list includes: Karluk River, Situk River, Kvichak River, Naknek River, Talarik Creek, Ugashik, and of course, Kenai River, and Susitna River.

In my opinion, these are the ten most popular. Many will challenge my opinion, giving valid reasons for including their favorite. On any given day, I, too, may select differently. I have fished with guides who have taken me to their secret spots where I have enjoyed Alaska's best. I respect their trust in sharing their hard-earned and sometimes expensive discovery. Some special streams, and even sections of streams, I have found on my own, and I'm selfishly keeping them to myself. Every angler should have their own, secret Alaska fishing hole.

I had the urge to tell what my favorite river is, but decided against it. I have not fished my favorite stream for three years. The last time I was there I got skunked, but it was an enjoyable trip with a group of old friends. It was more of a reunion than a serious fishing outing. It's not the size or numbers of fish that make the memories, it's who you're with.

Top Ten Lures

Manufacturers make their lures for fishermen, not fish," the clerk commented as my fishing buddy, loaded with a zillion kinds and colors headed for the checkout counter. I had just met Rick, a first-time Alaska angler. He had saved his money for several years and was at the beginning of his once-in-a-lifetime trip to Alaska. We came together through a group of mutual friends and for the next week we would be floating and fishing a remote Alaska river. Rick, not wanting to be in the bush without the proper lure, stopped by the local tackle store and loaded up on terminal tackle. Had he asked me what he should take to the river instead of asking the clerk, his tackle box would not have contained nearly the variety of lures, sizes, or colors, nor would he have hauled so many back to California when his trip was over.

Early in my Alaska fishing career I fished strictly with Dardevles. My tackle box was loaded with several different weights and as many different colors. My thinking was I would do better if I used the lure I was most familiar with and just changed the color or size as water clarity, depth, and current velocity demanded. I did pretty well and caught at least my share.

Then my fishing habits changed and I began fishing with guides and discovered a new world of lures. Almost every guide had his favorite lure which he considered his secret weapon. When the fishing slowed he'd dig in his bag of tricks and produce a strange new lure, claiming, "This one will break the curse. It always does. Just wait and see."

They'll usually bring out one of the top ten lures for Alaska.

Here's what I've learned guides consider the top ten lures in order of preference: Pixies, Dardevles, Spin-N-Glos, salmon eggs, Tee Spoons, Mepps spinners, Tad Pollys, Rooster Tails, Vibrax, and Krocodiles. I'm convinced I need them all and my tackle box contains some of all ten. I listen to the guides and tackle store experts and accept their advice, hook, line, and sinker.

Volcano Bay Silvers

The Aleutian Islands are hauntingly beautiful and uncommonly picturesque. The Aleutians are a different world. A thick, emerald-green blanket covers the surrounding mountains and hills. Wildflowers are abundant. Visitors are entertained by bald eagles soaring overhead and sea otters playing in the bay.

Although all of the above is true, the Aleutians are also a different world for worldly-wise anglers and those who seek the unusual, singular fishing experience. Alaska's fishing opportunities are unmatched anywhere, but occasionally a place or experience comes into a person's life that burns a memory deep in the brain. Volcano Bay is one of those places—at least for the present. Volcano Bay, untouched by the menacing nets of commercial fishing and even unblemished by subsistence practices, is a small angling area where you can go today and fish where legions upon legions of fish rush to their procreative destiny.

I experienced only the silvers of Volcano Bay. The day I spent throwing a fly over the waves of a rolling surf to running salmon is high on my list of memory grabbers. Like a volcano eruption, sea-fresh Volcano Bay silver salmon distinguish themselves by striking with enthusiasm and running with their legendary and celebrated full strength. Volcano Bay, like many Aleutian salmon streams, is untouched by commercial fishing. Fishing Volcano Bay has just got to be silver salmon's grand slam.

My time at Volcano Bay began with a short floatplane flight from Unalaska in a turbine deHavilland Beaver. Volcano Bay's Hawaii-like appearance, complete with lofty, prominent, volcanic peak backdrop and striking white sand beach, stuns the senses. If it were not for glaciers hanging from distant ridges, I would have thought I was a visitor to the South Pacific. The day I spent at Volcano bay, the weather was like it was imported from Waikiki.

My companions were Greg Hawthorne, owner of Volcano Bay Lodge, and fishing guide and charter captain John Lucking. My purpose was to film these two expert anglers fly-fishing the surf for silvers for a future episode of the Alaska Outdoors television show. It was almost like watching a ballet as these two followed the receding waves, cast as far as they could into the ocean, retreated up the beach before running waves while stripping line from their reels, and then retrieved their line in the traditional manner of fly-fishing. More often than not the acrobatic species are tough fighters. Volcano Bay silvers are some of the toughest. The direction of their run was unpredictable. Some charged directly toward the angler while using the rushing surf to jet-propel them free of the hook. Others ran parallel to the beach, catching the waves like experienced surfboarders, using the rolling water to leverage their already powerful plunge for escape. Some caught a receding wave and found their freedom by pulling away with the help of 3- and 4-foot waves. Others, not so lucky, succumbed to John's and Greg's experience.

John and Greg didn't actually land their catch; they beached it. I watched as they got the tired salmon taking the easy way toward the beach deep within a wave. Once the wave expended its energy on the white sand and returned to the sea, the anglers would hold tight while the receding water left the fish high and dry. John and Greg would then rush and try to bring the fish to high ground before a returning wave captured their catch. Most of the time they were successful. Occasionally they got wet and the silver either escaped or began another fight.

Late in the afternoon, when the picture taking was finished, Greg lent me his rod and I tried to duplicate his ballet. My form wouldn't match his, but the result equaled his when a silver struck and headed for Kodiak. Even after watching Greg and John battle the Volcano Bay silvers, I wasn't prepared for the strength of the charge for freedom and was quickly left with an empty hook. Several times silvers came out ahead before I was able to hold one while the waves returned to the sea and left my prize lying on the sand.

My day at Volcano Bay was mostly watching and filming, a little fishing, but above all, probably the most memorable one-day fishing outing in my life.

Deer Hair Mouse

One of the reasons I consented to fish the Goodnews River with Mike Gorton was his tantalizing tales of taking sockeye salmon on a deer hair mouse fly. Most anglers agree that reds are finicky feeders when in fresh water. Many anglers simply state, "reds never bite." Then comes Mike Gorton, owner of Goodnews River Lodge with, "We take 'em on a deer hair mouse all the time. He so convinced me that I was willing to try.

After I arrived at the lodge, Mike backpedaled a bit by qualifying his previous sure-deal brag "We do it all the time when conditions are right."

"What conditions?" I inquired.

"Find 'em in shallow water or close to the top. It's best if you find two males fighting each other for a nest," Mike replied. "Water's a bit high right now, but I still think you can do it."

I looked Mike straight in the eye. His eyes met mine and there was a glimmer that said he was telling the truth so I took the bait. "Can we try it tomorrow," I asked.

It seemed to me that Mike made sure a few of the guides were listening before he answered. "Any time you want, just ask your guide."

The first day's fishing was spent getting acquainted with the river, but toward afternoon I asked my guide if we could go for a red on a deer hair mouse. He agreed, but added, "I know they do it all the time but I've never caught a red on a deer hair and I'm not sure of the way to do it. We can try." His straight face suggested his answer was genuine.

After an hour of scaring sockeye out of their intended nests by tossing a mouse over their heads and dragging it back trying to imitate a mouse swimming for his life, I gave up and we headed back to the lodge.

The next morning I had a different guide. Yes, he would be glad to take me to a spot where he thought we could connect, but then added, "I've never done it, but Mike does all the time and he's told me how." Then he gave me a grin suggesting he's wasn't convinced.

The only change to the water-flaying exercise of the previous day was the length of time spent throwing the mouse at a group of reds. The day before I'd given it only an hour. This day, I doubled the time, but with the same results—nothing—not one rise. The guide did tell me a time or two that one of the targeted fish followed the swimming mouse-looking fly, but I only saw reds moving away. On the way back to the lodge in the evening I started to wonder why the guide didn't pick up a rod and test his mettle since he admitted earlier that he hadn't ever done it before.

By morning the thought of the guide not picking up a rod had disappeared when my guide for the day admitted to having taken a red on a mouse. After I spent two hours of good fishing time with a mouse and no results, and the guide didn't pick up his rod, for some reason I remembered a snipe hunt. You know, where the one who has never hunted snipe before is left alone in the woods holding a flashlight in a bag while those who have hunted before go out and beat the bushes and scare the snipe into the bag.

By morning I'd worked up enough courage to suggest to Mike that his red on a deer hair mouse was probably a snipe hunt. "No way," he said. "We do it all the time. You'll connect today and if you don't, I'll personally take you tomorrow."

Well, I didn't connect. Two more hours of dragging a mouse in little jerking motions across the top of reds in deep water and shallow. "Are you sure this isn't a snipe hunt?" I asked Mike when we returned.

"Course it's not a snipe hunt," he said. "Tomorrow we'll find the right hole."

Later that night I heard some of the guides laughing in one of their cabins and I just knew I was the reason. I could just hear them talking and laughing about this guy who's been in Alaska for 44 years being taken on a red salmon snipe hunt.

I was ready to tell Mike the snipe hunt's off and let's just go fishing when he showed up with his personal $1,000 rod and reel with a deer hair mouse already attached to the tippet. "Let's go catch a red," he proclaimed.

The drill with Mike was no different than with the other guides. I threw the fly, they encouraged from the sideline, but didn't pick up a rod and show me how it was done. Finally, Mike said, "I guess the water's too high or the hole's too crowded or something's wrong. Let's just go fishing."

And like the days before, we fished. It was fishing out of this world and it took the edge off the deer hair snipe hunt. As the day ended, which was my last day to fish the Goodnews, I said to Mike, "Okay Mike, I've gone every day on your snipe hunt. I've heard the guides laugh at night, and my arm's sore from casting your long rod to reds. Now tell me the truth. It's a snipe hunt, right?"

"It's no snipe hunt. Reds will take a deer hair mouse. You can believe it. It's no snipe hunt. It's for real."

"Okay" I said. "Play it all the way. Play it to the end."

"Evan," Mike said. "I'd never take you on a snipe hunt. We just didn't find the right conditions. I can give you names and phone numbers of at least a dozen guys who've been here and taken reds on a mouse."

Mike seemed hurt that I didn't believe him so I let it drop. Late that night I again heard the guides laughing from their tents. But that's alright. They'd sure shown me a good time and put me on plenty of fish, and I learned a few tricks from these pros. So I just put it down as part of the price of admission.

As I was leaving, Mike shook my hand and expressed good feelings, and extended an invitation to "come back again, anytime." And the last thing I remember him saying, "And next time, we'll take a sockeye on a mouse."

Now that I'm back home and have had a chance to think about my week on the Goodnews, I remember that everything about my trip was just like Mike said it would be—and maybe more. Perhaps he wasn't pulling my leg. Maybe it wasn't a snipe hunt.

And then I remember his "Come back again, anytime" invitation. Okay Mike. I'll come back. "Let's go fish for reds on a fly." I don't care if it's a snipe hunt or not, and I don't care if the guides laugh at me every night. A couple of hours of mouse-at-reds fishing is a small price to pay for a day's fishing in water created in heaven for a fly fisherman. I'll even pretend that I'm hopeful I'll score with a mouse. You keep asking me back and I'll keep throwing a mouse at sockeye. When I think about it in this perspective I get to wondering, who's on the snipe hunt, me or Mike?

Fishing Evolution

My first fishing outing was up Oak Creek Canyon with Uncle Ivan on opening day of trout season. The fishing equipment consisted of a 10-foot cane pole with electric tape wrapped around the butt to form a makeshift handle. Attached to the pole was a line with a small loop tied on the free end. An Eagle Claw hook with a 12-inch store-bought leader containing a loop of approximately the same size as the one on the line was fastened to the line by locking the loops together. A used pork'n bean can full of nightcrawlers rounded out the outfit.

Paralleling each other for several miles, the road and Oak Creek came close together numerous times, and a one-car parking spot developed where fishermen had easy access to water. Uncle Ivan parked below the big springs. He knew it was here where the Fish and Game truck, which had stocked the stream several days earlier, made its last stop dumping what remained of its load. Uncle Ivan was acquainted with the warden who patrolled the canyon for poachers and the warden had advised this would be the best fishing spot.

The hole was under the bridge. We stood upriver and let our nightcrawler-laden Eagle Claw hook bounce along the bottom with the current. As soon as the bait hit the top of the hole, we had a strike. The fight consisted of setting the hook and landing the 10-inch hatchery-raised rainbow with one jerk. In less than an hour a 20-fish limit was taken, killed, and cleaned. Mom fixed a fresh fish feast for breakfast the next few days.

My first step up in fishing equipment was prior to a boy scout fishing and camping super summer activity when I purchased, with my own money, a steel telescoping rod and matching level wind reel. Eight seasons I packed it into high mountain lakes for cutthroat trout, tied it to the handle bars of my bike to get to the local rainbow streams, and carried it on the bus to Yellowstone to fish the Madison and Fire Hole Rivers. The rod gave good service until it was retired when I moved to Alaska.

My arrival in Alaska was timed with the introduction of fiberglass and spinning reels. A Mitchell 300 became the status symbol as I entered the world of subsistence salmon fishing. The pork'n beans can of night crawlers was exchanged for a tackle box full of Mepps, Tee Spoons, and flash bait. Six salmon was the limit with a two-day possession limit. Habitually I would catch a limit before midnight and another one after. Beginning with the red run, our family diet rotated from moose and caribou to fried, baked, broiled, and smoked fish.

Concurrent with a gift of a fly-fishing outfit, I was introduced to catch and release. With fly-fishing came the necessity of an increased quantity of fishing paraphernalia: pliers, chest waders, fishing vest, twist-on weights, and the list went on. My fly rod gift was a four-section pack rod. Its first tour of duty produced an 8-pound, distinctly rainbow, rainbow on the first cast when fishing the Talachulitna River. I freely confess to enjoying releasing the fish to fight again. Imagining a now larger and wiser fish haunting the holes added a new and enjoyable perspective to later outings on the Tal.

The next stage in my fishing finishing school found me leaving the fly rod and fishing vest home, substituting a Canon camera and Kodachrome 64 film. A new element of catch and release emerged as I now release and keep. Keep on film.

Recently, the after-dinner fishing lodge conversation turned to fishing reels as a fellow angler touted the qualities of his newly purchased fly reel. Each person around the table hefted and admired the precision craftsmanship and tooling. As my turn for inspection arrived and I held the instrument, its owner announced the reel's $1,200 price tag.

Before retiring I contemplated where I was on the fishing evolution chart. Determining I was about in the middle, halfway between the can of nightcrawlers and a $1,200 hand-made reel, I could not tell for sure which way on the chart I was going and I didn't care. As long as I can be on the bank near the water, I'll take either the pork'n bean can, the steel telescoping rod, or the handcrafted reel. It makes no difference to me if I'm catching with a hook or capturing with a camera. It's fishing.

Fishing fun is no respecter of age, price, or position. It's just right wherever you are. I'm thankful my lot fell where I can fish Alaska.

The Fishing Hole

On the Homer Spit I witnessed a group of inexperienced and uninformed anglers fishing in the Fishing Hole. They threw the correct lure and used the proper technique for several discouraging hours. They knew the kings were there. They could see them jump and occasionally someone would snag one and have it on for a moment. After awhile, in frustration, they would leave the water—depressed with their ability to duplicate what they knew others had done. Then the tide changed, fish moved in, smart anglers arrived, and for an hour the fishing matched Alaska's reputation. The tide peaked, the hole cooled, and the unfortunate, uninformed, upon hearing of great fishing, returned, only to be discouraged further.

If you're going to fish the Homer Spit's Fishing Hole get a tide book. Don't start fishing until the tide begins to come in. You'll notice water coming into the lagoon—then start fishing. I recommend you fish the west end. The best method appears to be to use a float, followed by a 3-foot leader with a single hook, and herring for bait. As soon as you set the hook, try to get your catch to shore as quickly as possible. Once the king realizes he's hooked he'll put up a considerably more difficult fight. You won't require a net. Your fellow anglers will have one and will be more than willing to help you land your catch.

When the tide turns in the Fishing Hole you may want to drive to Stariski Creek for fish action of a different kind. Bring your camera at low tide. Conceal yourself and your photography equipment in the trees and underbrush near the mouth. Almost every low tide leaves a few kings struggling in shallow water. The area is home to several eagles who use shallow water and low tide to hunt for their dinner. These eagles circle, waiting for the right time, and then swoop and attack a struggling king. The bird is not large enough to fly off with its prey, but they are able to drag it to shore and quickly dispatch it. Then it shares it with its family and friends. The whole exercise provides the observer with an excellent photo opportunity and a lasting memory of the national bird taking Alaska's most sought-after fish out to lunch.

Thanks to the Men

The 14-year-old boy approached the bank of Pelican Creek with caution. Standing on tiptoes, he was able to see over the edge to the water. The water was clear, and coming over his shoulder, the sun penetrated the surface, exposing the largest trout the boy had ever seen. With his heart pounding in his chest loud enough to scare the fish away, he quickly set up the steel telescoping fishing rod and put a night crawler on the Eagle Claw hook.

The youthful angler was not wearing the traditional fishing clothes. He wore hiking boots, faded blue jeans, and a dark green shirt. On the sleeves and pockets of his shirt were patches from the organization he was a member of. They were not from Trout Unlimited, Fly Fishing Federation, or the local fishing association. One large patch identified the wearer as a member of a Boy Scouts of America troop. Smaller ones designated skills earned or camps attended.

Pelican Creek, in Yellowstone park, is several hundred miles from the boy's home. Standing behind and encouraging the fisherman is his scoutmaster. Scoutmaster Hap Glad had encouraged and helped him earn the money to join the troop on their summer super activity: ten days of wilderness camping and fishing.

Getting ready for the excursion was an event in itself. Camping, cooking, first aid, and swimming skills were taught, learned and demonstrated. Merit badges were earned and advancement in rank achieved. Saturday night fund-raising movie tickets were sold, newspapers were collected, doughnuts delivered, and lawns mowed and raked. The money was earned, how to work was learned.

Now wearing the badges of achievement on his chest, the young man is about to attempt to catch a fish almost as long as his arm. Knowing if he gets too close the trout will spook makes the boy stop 10 feet short of the water's edge. He doesn't want to cast his shadow on the water. His arm is shaking so much he can hardly throw the rod. The cast is six feet too long. Before he can retrieve the bait and throw again, the fish turns and eyes the night crawler. It is evident the trout can see the worm in the clear water.

Scouter Hap Glad coaches from the rear. "Don't move," he whispers. He had been coaching the scout for several months. Helping him raise the funds and earn the awards. Shorter overnight hikes in the mountains and camps on the lakes were taken. The young man is now at home in the woods sleeping in a tent, and comfortable eating his own cooking from a campfire. A positive self-image has developed through working to earn his own way and achieving his awards presented at the Court of Honors.

Every muscle in the boy's body is tense and tight. The fish sizes up the bait for what seems like an eternity. Its tail and fins move, keeping it sideways in the creek's current. Slowly it moves forward about two feet and then stops again. The once pounding heart of the scout seems to also stop. Then the fish makes its decision. With a burst of color, the trout charges the bait like a lightning bolt.

This is why the boy had hiked eight miles with his heavy pack. Why he had spent nearly every Saturday for five months raising funds. Why he worked so hard to learn outdoor skills and fishing techniques.

In a fraction of a second it was over. Taut nerves and youthful impatience caused the young angler to set the hook before the strike was complete. The bait and hook came out of the water empty. The fish, now knowing something was wrong, headed for cover.

What his scoutmaster told the disappointed boy is lost to memory. What is remembered are the lessons and the love for the outdoors retained. I know. I thank God for leaders like Hap Glad and for the Boy Scouts of America. I am grateful for fresh air, for forested mountains, for camping, for fishing, and for other outdoor activities. I hope every boy can belong to a scout troop and have a scoutmaster who cares and teaches.

That was the last time I set the hook before a fish took the bait.

Take a Kid Fishing

Jesse learned to cast before he could walk. My first recollection of fishing with him is one of me standing in hip waders in Otto Lake with Jesse sitting on my shoulders. We were fishing for grayling. He would cast off our right side and I would cast to the left. More often than not we would have doubles on.

The last week in May I took the kid fishing again. We upgraded the drive to the river, a camp-out, do-it-yourself fishing trip to a drive to the lodge, fully guided, someone-else-do-the-work fishing experience. The early run of saltwater kings bound for the Kenai River and Upper Cook Inlet were our target.

We stayed at Trophy King Lodge, about 28 miles north of Homer, on the beach between the Sterling Highway and Cook Inlet. Our guide was Mike Constant. It was cold when we left in the boats for the fishing spot.

As do all good guides, Mike had a story to tell until a king hit, then it wouldn't matter what the weather was, we would be warm. Mike said his dad told him you can't catch if you are comfortable. We were cold and uncomfortable and we were not catching fish. Mike got Jesse laughing and warmed him up a bit when he said, "If what my dad said was true, this morning I would sit on the side of my pocketknife to make the fishing pick up." Not long after, we took the first hit, then another, and then the third. A triple hit. As the battle raged, we fought to get the fish in without tangling lines. Mike held up his knife and told Jesse, "I guess I had better put my pocketknife away." I can't remember what the weather was like for the rest of the day.

That morning our boat of four fishermen boated nine kings in a 3-hour run on the high tide. We had many others hooked but could not complete the job. Several were close enough to the net when they finally shook the hook that the guide would call it catch and release. Mike named it LDR—long distance release.

King salmon are born into the world without knowing their parents and die without meeting their children. This may be the reason why they fight so hard. Perhaps they are mad for being raised orphans and dying before their children are born. At any rate, when hooked in salt water they seem to have a mad on and are determined to take it out on the hook. Since the hook is attached to a line connected to a rod and reel held by a thrill-seeking angler, the battle for freedom brings sore arms, a tired back, and heart-pounding, stress-erasing, and soul-relaxing recreation.

The limit in Cook Inlet is five kings per season. Keeping three apiece for the locker and Sunday dinner, we released the balance. The last of May left a lot of season before us and we did not want to fill our tags this early in the year.

At week's end Jesse went home drunken with fresh, clean, clear salt air, suntanned cheeks, and the overall intoxication that comes from being in the outdoors catching fish with his dad.

The kid is 30 years older than on our first trip to Otto lake.

Some Things Never Change

It was the spring of '58 on Twenty-Mile Creek along Turnagain Arm that our family first found hooligan. Hooligan fishing was also my first Alaska outing with a resident fishing license in my pocket. I wish I'd kept it. It was the only one I received from the Territory of Alaska since the following year Alaska was admitted as a state in the United States.

Hooligan, called candlefish by some, are smelt which run with regularity up Turnagain Arm in the spring. Catching hooligan is accomplished by wading into the stream until your hip boots or waders are one quarter of an inch taller than the water depth. Using a long-handled dip net, hooligan anglers scoop up the little fish as they school up the river. Bag limits for hooligan are generous and catching them on the incoming tide quickly fills the angler's bucket, cooler, or other container.

Our first hooligan trip proved to be more than an angling outing, it became a picnic and social gathering where we met new friends doing the same thing we were—using these little fish as an excuse to break our cabin fever and head to the wilderness—even if the wilderness was along the highway and almost in the town of Portage.

We dipped until four things happened all at once: we filled our tag, went semi-hypothermic when we got careless and waded too deep for our boots, we ran out of sandwiches and hot chocolate, and the tide turned.

We took our catch home and tried every recipe given us by hooligan lovers. We tried them all with the same results—tasteless dinners.

The last time I was on Turnagain Arm in the spring, I witnessed hordes of Alaska newcomers standing in ice-cold incoming tide water catching a hooligan or two and filling their waders as the tide came up and the angler dipped low. Kids ran around on the mud flats and consumed sandwiches and hot chocolate, and cried because they got cold and wet. Soon the tide changed and most people left to clean their catch and try newly discovered recipes. Yep, some things never change.

Another thing that never changes about hooligan fishing—I'll wager a box of light bulbs against a bucket of candle fish that the new-to-Alaska anglers I saw along Turnagain did the same thing I did four decades ago—tried all the recipes, didn't like any of them, and after weighing the cost to benefits came up with the same conclusion I did on my first hooligan outing—I'd enjoy hooligan fishing henceforth as a watcher and that first hooligan fishing trips are also last hooligan fishing trips.

Rod Holder in the New Boat

It was a cool day early in May. We were fishing about a mile below the Sterling Highway Bridge. Fishing with a barbless hook, Lars allowed his first steelhead of the day to escape. Lars called it catch and release, but Ken Robertson, the guide, muttered something about, "LDR. Long distance release." Lars's second strike came in the form of an underwater snag that swallowed his lure and kept it.

Lars accused Ken of giving him a rebellious lure. Ken said Lars didn't know how to fish. "Your knots are weak," was Lars's response. "The lure just fell off. I hardly pulled at all."

"If you'd pulled any harder, the rod would have busted," was Ken's retort. "I know how to tie knots; you just don't know how to fish."

"Why don't you throw your old, worn-out lures away instead of giving them to me for bait?"

"Old lures? Lars, that was a brand-new $25 super special that can't be replaced. It was one of a kind."

The friendly heckling continued. "Get in the tackle box, pick your own lure, and tie it on for yourself."

Lars rose to the challenge and selected what he called "the best of Ken's bad lures." A light blue one. Used. Almost abused. He joked about Ken not having anything worthwhile as he looked over the tackle box freshly stocked with the latest lures. The box was filled to the brim and well organized in preparation for the coming season, but Lars ignored this and continued with the one-liners.

"What'd you do Ken, spend all your money on the new boat, and now can't afford lures?"

"I save that kind of terminal tackle for people who can't fish. It don't make sense to give novices new, expensive stuff. They'd just lose it on a snag."

By now Lars had the little blue Wiggle Wart firmly fastened and dropped it behind the boat, letting the line out four passes on the reel as Ken had instructed.

"You're not really fishing, Lars. I'm doing the fishing. You're a rod holder. You just hold the rod and I put it into the hole where the fish are."

Ken was rowing back and forth across the river, inching his way into each hole. Ken's steelhead philosophy is you've got to hunt them out, stay with them, and put it right in their face. If there are fish in the hole, they'll have a chance to at least look at the lure.

"Well, put me into a fish, Ken."

"You've got a fish, Lars."

"It's another snag."

"No. It's a fish."

"It's not going anywhere. It must have hung up again."

"Well if it did, it now broke loose and it's swimming upstream. Set the hook."

All of a sudden the jokes and heckling stopped. Lars became a steelhead angler and Ken, the old master guide, coached his client. Combination of skill and guide instruction soon subdued the steelhead and Ken brought out the net. For a moment, there was peace in the boat as both men concentrated on landing the sea-run rainbow. As soon as the fish was in the boat it began again.

"You make a good rod holder, even if you are a rod holder that talks back."

Rainbow Bay

Nearly everyone hearing about Rainbow Bay Resort jumps to the conclusion the lodge's namesake is the resident fish taken right off the end of the dock. Not so. The next obvious thought, still about fishing, is the lodge's proximity to native rainbow waters. Wrong again. The name has nothing to do with fishing.

Fishing the Iliamna River out of Rainbow Bay Resort, Brett Huber's bait hit bottom and started to drift. Different from the earlier drifts, this one began to move directly toward the fisherman. He cranked his reel to take up the slack in the line. Directly in front of him, with only 12 feet still out, the line tightened. Now, the business end of the line took off for deep water, the rest of the line following, making fisherman's music with the reel. Brett was sure he had a red. In the second his mind took to decide it was a sockeye, 40 feet of line was peeled off the reel.

Without warning, the end of the line reversed, and began moving back toward the angler. Then, in typical rainbow fashion, 10 feet from Brett, the fish broke the surface, twisting, turning, and shaking in an effort to dislodge the hook. With the knowledge that the fish was a rainbow and twice as big as the last one he had just released, his heart pumped faster, and his cold hands began to sweat.

Now, all his senses were alert and his fishing skill was brought out. The rainbow made run after run, jump after jump. It had missed escaping on the first try, more by fisherman good fortune than skill, and now Brett was in the lead. Twenty minutes after it began, Brett was holding for the camera the largest rainbow trout he had ever caught.

The release was performed with almost sacred ritual. It's not every day a fisherman is granted the opportunity to overcome man's ancient desire to kill for food, and release a trophy back to the rainbow gods of the lake.

He had been to the mountain. He was on a high. For now, at least, anything less than an 8-pound rainbow would be a comedown. Knowing that every cast would desecrate the experience, Brett put away his equipment, sat on shore with his face directly into the dying wind, and pondered the moment.

Breaking through the clouds over the mountains to the west, sunlight burst across Lake Iliamna with searchlight-like rays, lighting up the hills to the east of Rainbow Bay. Light rain had replaced the wind-driven downpour of the morning. Moisture-laden air, and horizontal beams of the setting sun combined to produce a ground-to-ground rainbow frame over the lodge. Mother Nature had confirmed the true reason for the name of this part of Lake Iliamna, and for the sign on the lodge that reads Rainbow Bay.

Florette C

The Florette C doesn't look like any charter boat I've been on and the captain is also quite different—she's a lady, Dianne Debuk. The boat doesn't have the traditional rack on back with broomstick-like halibut rods hanging overhead. Other boats' decks are flat at the back, allowing six anglers to belly up to the rail while fishing. A 5-foot-square, 2-foot-high hatch occupies the Florette C's deck's center and opens to a large hold underneath.

The hold, unused for its original purpose, contains odds and ends, everything from spray paint to garden hoses. Anglers not fishing can comfortably sit on the hatch cover or on a fold-out deck chair placed on deck between the hatch and a utility tower near the boat's stern. The utility tower functions as a communication radio antenna base, as the boat's second power and steering control center, and holds brackets for fishing rods.

At the edge of the boat's stern, instead of the traditional rail, there's a 3-foot deep well where two anglers stand level with the ocean and tend two fishing rods apiece. Most charters allow six anglers to fish at once giving this type of fishing the six-pack title. Not so with the Florette C. Six anglers rotate in teams of two for 20 minutes of fishing. At first blush it seems to cut down on the fishing time, but given the way Dianne fishes her clients, it may cut down on the fishing time, but it increases the catching time.

The Florette C is a Southeast Alaska commercial troller converted to a luxury sportfishing yacht complete with long trolling poles on either side of the boat and hydraulically powered downriggers.

And this is where Regina Monaco took her first fish—her first two fish. Alaska newcomer and TV reporter, Regina was filling her assignment of covering Alaska's sportfishing arena, without ever having been fishing before. Fortunately for Regina, her charter boat captain, Dianne Debuk, had been fishing, and provided Regina with, not only the fishing technique lessons, but the opportunity to apply the newly learned knowledge on two feeder kings and a respectable halibut.

Like most novice anglers, Regina couldn't keep the rod tip up, let the line go slack, and made all the other mistakes, allowing fish to escape. But again as with most novice anglers, the fish gods took pity and allowed the mistakes, and the fish to be taken. So it was with Regina. She took her trophies home to dinner and her TV report to the nightly news broadcast.

When asked about her first Alaska fishing experience, her first two fish, and the ultimate charter aboard Alaska Saltwater Charters' Florette C and lady captain, Dianne Debuk, Regina answered with one word—the meaningless word that means much to many—awesome!

Florette C Species Specific

The last angler on board the Florette C arrived at exactly the designated departure time. Even before introductions could be extended, Captain Dianne Debuk was detailing the features of her boat, Coast Guard safety requirements, the location of snacks, and the lunch menu. It was a beautiful, early March morning. Winds were calm; the sun's first rays were creeping over glacier-dotted hills to the east of Homer's small boat harbor on the spit. Although El Niño influenced, the warmer-than-usual morning's small breeze still had a bite to it and the cabin's warmth felt good as Dianne motored her craft into the open sea.

The latecomer approached the helm observing a bank of the latest fishing and electronic safety gear. Near the center of the console was a small, famed photograph of a lovely lady. Captain Debuk noticed the latecomer's question before it was asked.

"That's my mother. She goes with me on every trip. I talked to her on the telephone last night. Told her you placed an order for clear skies, flat water, and fish. I've known for years she has a direct connection with the man upstairs and I asked her to pray so we could fill your order." Dianne was laughing when she talked about her mother, but the latecomer could tell she had a sense of believing her own story.

Just down the bay from Soldovia, Dianne slowed the boat and announced, "Get ready to fish." Those on the charter who were regulars knew Dianne meant draw cards to see who fishes first. A 2-foot wide fishing compartment ran along the entire back of the Florette C. The all-wood boat had spent most of its life as a salmon troller in Southeast Alaska, but was now retired to sportfishing. Long poles extended 20 feet on either side. Two downriggers wearing 30-pound cannon balls were attached to a pulley system via steel cable to the poles. The cannon balls' depth was controlled by a simple hydraulic system. As the cannon ball sank deeper marks appeared along the cable notifying the operator of the depth. At predetermined marks fishing line was attached to the cable by a clothespin-like device. The terminal end was a foot-long flasher followed by a small hook encased in a 3-inch herring attached commercial-troller-like, not like a conventional sportfishing charter would fix its bait.

The latecomer drew an ace, and one of the regulars a jack, winning them the first chance to fish. Dianne's deckhand handled baiting and rigging the lines as Dianne maneuvered her boat near the rock face where she intended to troll. As the first line reached the sought-for depth a telltale jerk developed at the rod's end. The latecomer set the hook and the deckhand knowingly announced, "small halibut."

The latecomer cranked his catch aboard as the deckhand rigged and positioned the other three rods. The first team fished their allotted time and continued to boat or release a string of halibut catches, but no kings, the real target for the day. And so went the second and third shifts. No kings, just small halibut.

When the latecomer and his partner's time came for their second try they joked,. "Let's get off this halibut kick." And they did. One after another tom cod came aboard, were cursed, and quickly released. But no kings. The other teams experienced a similar catching and releasing.

As the latecomer and his teammate started third shift, Dianne came to the boat's back and wished them luck. In passing, the latecomer quipped to Dianne, "Next time ask your mother to be species specific. We're catching fish, but next time ask her to order kings."

"Okay, that's the problem?" asked Dianne. "Well, catch a king."

"Fish on! "shouted the latecomer's teammate.

"King on," said Dianne, knowing and reading the wiggle on the rod tip.

The king was boated and then another and the ice was broken even for the other teams. The fishing day was a success and topped off with a bonus when the Florette C stopped and pulled crab pots laid out earlier.

The next time Captain Dianne Debuk asks her mother to talk to the man upstairs, she'll undoubtedly be species specific.

Florette C Pray for Fish

Morning fog was just giving way to the sun's burning rays as I walked the dock's finger to the waiting Florette C. Dianne Debuk, the boat's captain, told me over the phone the day before, "Be at the dock at 7:30, Ramp 1 C, space 10. We'll leave immediately for feeder kings."

Feeders are not the return-to-the-natal-stream monsters like those which run to the Kenai in summer months. Feeders are transients. They may have been born in Russia or Canada and just spend both summer and winter feeding off the shores of Alaska and growing fat and mature for their return to their river of birth, whether it be domestic or foreign.

Although they invade the waters of Kachemak Bay without a passport, they are welcomed by adventure-seeking anglers, and I'm one of them. Saltwater fishing is not my favorite. I'd much rather be fly-fishing a small clear-water tributary of Fish River for arctic grayling than dragging a line off the bottom of the ocean. But if I want feeder kings, I must go down to the sea in a ship. That's where the feeders are.

In Southeast Alaska they call 'em shakers. Over in Prince William Sound they're known as winter kings. In Kachemak Bay, most folks know them as feeders. By and large, feeders are smaller than spawners. A 35-pound feeder is a big fish, but an occasional 50-pounder may be taken. Most are in the 20-pound class. However, what they lack in size, they make up for in heart. They're fighters to the last flip of the tail.

Many feeder king guides will not allow anglers to release their catch simply because the fish has totally exhausted itself in its fight for freedom and hasn't the strength to survive beyond the challenge it gave the angler. Sometimes a small feeder is quickly overpowered by the rod and reel and may be safely released. Most times the angler is anxious to put his newly caught feeder in the boat's fish box anyway. If you've ever eaten a feeder you'd know why. They're the best. There's no other fish like 'em.

And so it was that I came to Kachemak Bay with feeders on my mind. The tide was out and the walk down the approach to the boat ramp was more of a climb down to the boat ramp. At least I knew that when I returned, hopefully carrying a load of fish, the tide would be in and the climb with a heavy load would be easier.

No sooner did I round the corner and spot the Florette C, than the deck hand spotted me and and notified Captain Debuk. She was at the rail welcoming me and giving safety instructions almost before I was fully aboard. My gear wasn't even stored in the cabin before Dianne was backing out and heading for the open water.

I wondered what the rush was. It was barely 7:30, our scheduled departure time. Later I learned that Captain Debuk has a passion for feeders and sitting at the dock gives her symptoms of feeder withdrawal, satisfied only by getting her client's line in the water. Mostly, she's a happy, pleasant lady, but there's a decidedly different aura about her person when she's close to land from when she's at sea with clients.

The Florette C is a converted commercial salmon troller from Southeast Alaska. Amid radar screens, depth finders, compasses, GPS, and other electronic gear is a faded picture of a lady resembling Captain Debuk.

Upon inquiring who the person was, Dianne confirmed that the distinguished-looking lady was her mother, Florette, for whom the boat was named.

Dianne says she likes to have her mother close to her as she plies the ocean in search of fish. In fact, Dianne said, "I talked to her this morning. Told her I was going out for fish and asked her to pray that we'd catch some."

"Can't you do your own praying?" I jested.

"Oh sure," she said, "but mom seems to be closer to heaven and gets heard better than me. We'll catch fish today. Mom's prayed for us."

Captain Debuk was right. We caught fish. Feeders. Our limit of feeders. And more. A couple of halibut. And we pulled the boat's crab pots and scored big time. By the time the tide turned and the boat headed back to the Homer small boat harbor we'd had enough. At least enough for one day.

It was a great day. A new experience. A new friend. Several new friends. An experience I've enjoyed many times since, and we've always caught fish. But now the question. Is it the skill and knowledge of Captain Debuk? The expert way the unusual gear is used? Is it the time of year? Is it just luck? Probably all of the above. But I didn't ask the question I wanted to. What did Captain Dianne Debuk think? Was our good fortune due to her mother's prayer? If it was, I'm wondering if it'll work by all mothers, on all water, by all anglers. Maybe prayers are better than all the gear you can buy. And it's a whole lot cheaper.

Enid Brown's
First Fish on a Fly

Enid Brown, a Bering Sea Eskimo, has taken thousands of fish. As a young girl, growing up along the Fish River, she spent her summers in the fish camp. She was taught how to catch fish in a subsistence net by her mother and her grandmother. She had never fished with a fly rod and accepted my invitation to teach her the basics of casting.

About 200 yards before entering the Fish River, a small stream narrowed between a gravel bar and a high bank. The bank caused the water to form a series of S turns. At each turn a small holding pool was created. At the top of the first, yet unfished hole, a single grayling fed. Enid's first casts were short and poorly placed. Finally, she got the feeling and put a brown, woolly worm in the right spot. She could see the fly drift with the current, heading for the fish's mouth. Anticipation built to a crescendo in the few seconds it took for the bait to get to the fish. The offering was refused. Twice more Enid properly placed the fly at the top of the hole and each time it was snubbed.

I suggested the fish had poor eyesight and she try a bright yellow woolly worm. It received the same lack of interest. The yellow was easier for us to see in the water and presumably easier for the fish. Each time it drifted through the sweet spot of the hole, the grayling moved over and let it pass. Five times it refused.

Enid thought we should move down to the next hole. I asked her to try a green woolly worm and tied one on for her. By now her skill at casting was improving and she could hit the current at the top of the hole with regularity. The green presentation was received with like disdain.

I tried to keep the new fly-fisherman's interest up by suggesting we try a black woolly worm. She complied, but with less enthusiasm. Her cast hit the edge of the current and drifted to the outside of the hole, missing the target by three feet. The fish spotted the bait, liked what it saw, and moved in for the kill. Like many grayling, it attacked from above. It came out of the water and dove on the fly. Enid's inexperience made her set the hook before the small mouth of the fish had completely encircled the fly. She felt pressure from the strike, but not enough to hold the fish and he escaped to the far side of the hole.

Enid's excitement was evidenced in her next two casts. The first one put the fly in the top of a small bush behind her. The second was a well-placed cast to her arm and she set the hook into her jacket. Finally she settled down, remembered her lessons, thought about her practice casts, and put the bait right on the money.

The fly caught the current perfectly to bring it and the fish together. Enid mended the line at the proper place and the imitation bug continued in its predestined path. The grayling came to the center of the hole and waited for the fly. The fish moved slowly toward the slowing bait. In the split second of the attack, the drift ended, the speed of the fly increased slightly by the crack-the-whip action of the line, and the fish missed the bait by a feather.

Either the grayling had a short memory or a determined constitution, for it came again on the next cast. What before had seemed to work against the fisherman, now combined to put it together. In a split second, flash and splash, Enid was battling her first fly-caught fish. Like all of us with our first fish, she forgot who she was and squealed like a schoolgirl out for recess. The fight was perfectly matched.

She was using a 3 1/2-ounce, 7-foot rod, with a floating line, and a 2-pound tippet. The battle continued with splash and dash by the fish and yell and squeal by Enid. It seemed to be a draw for several minutes, but fishing fights do not end in a tie. Finally the fisherman began to get the edge as the fish tired. Enid eased it into quite shallow water and picked it up for a photograph. Then, following the philosophy of the lodge, she released it back into the water. Anyone remembering their first fish on a fly rod can empathize with Enid's feelings of the moment. Enid will improve her skill and knowledge of fly-fishing and she will catch her first Dolly and her first salmon on a fly. Each will be exciting, but I wager my fishing hat, none will be more remembered than her first fish on a fly.

One in a Row

From reading books and writing reports as part of his school studies John Rosedale got the idea he wanted to come to Alaska . As John talked about Alaska, his father, Miles, conceived an idea for a father-son fishing outing. Miles's business schedule demanded him to fly monthly from his home in Arcadia, California to Oregon. These trips accomplished two things that brought about an Alaska fishing excursion. First it built up miles on his frequent flyer program which resulted in two free tickets to Alaska. Next, while on the airline he read articles and advertisements in magazines which gave him enough information to begin a search for a place to go. He sought a lodge which would be comfortable with a youngster in camp and would assist him and John in having a good time considering their limited ability as fishermen, and one that met his budget requirements. As Miles put it, "One that talked the most knowledgeable about fishing and not just bragging about the lodge."

After a time of reading, letter writing, and telephoning, father and son found the place they were looking for. They found one that seemed to know Alaska and appeared very knowledgeably about fish and fishing in the lodge's area. Reservations were made.

Through careful planning and a little luck all arrangements made by their travel agency were correct, their flights were on time, they were recognized and greeted by lodge personnel when they stepped off the plane, their luggage arrived with them, and the lodge itself was as they imagined it would be. Once in camp it took little time for the city to slip off, wilderness to slip on, cares of business and school to go away, and fishing to begin.

They backed-trolled Glory Hole and drifted Slough Hole for kings, had sockeye doubles on most of the time in the lower one third of the Fish and Game hole, lost the biggest fish of the trip in Cooks Hole, learned fly-fishing at Mosquito Point, got skunked in Aquarium Hole, and had their best day at Tin Shack Hole.

John landed his first fish in Alaska and his first salmon on a fly rod while fishing just off Mosquito Point. He was assisted by fellow fisherman Grant Petherick from Hasting, New Zealand. His father recorded the event with the camera to show Mom back home and for the benefit of any of John's doubting school friends.

Father and son agreed that their first trip to Alaska was just one in a row of many yet to come.

Newhalen River

Something got me thinking about fishing the Newhalen River. Although putting the trip together may require a bit more planning than a trip along the road system, it can be satisfying and within almost anyone's budget.

My first trip to the Newhalen River was in my old 1948 Stinson Voyager. My daughter, her friend, and her friend's father completed our party. We flew through scenic Lake Clark Pass and landed at Iliamna. We parked the plane off the edge of the east-west dirt runway and took the 45-minute hike to the river.

The river was choked with red salmon. They were stacked up like cordwood. It was impossible to bring in our line without a fish. If we had a hookup and it got off, another took its place. We soon had our limit of six salmon apiece filleted and packed for our hike back to the plane. The balance of the day was spent in fishing off the rocks for resident fish.

I was looking at the photographs of the trip recently and a flood of pleasant memories flowed across my mind. Here's how we made our memory, and any angler can duplicate our experience.

It's a little over a mile to the river. You can either camp off the cross-runway or carry your gear to the river. Once you get to the river you will see a group of rocks at the end of the river's fast water. You can fish from these rocks. Downriver from these rocks the river opens up into a wide delta. Immediately behind the rocks the fast water meets with still water of the delta and creates a long back eddy directly off the end of the rocks.

The best way I have found to fish here for resident fish is to stand on the rocks and cast as far as I can into the fast water of the main river. I let the current take my lure as far as it will before it swings into the back eddy. When the lure gets into the back eddy I stop my line from going out, move to the left side of the rocks, and begin as slow a retrieve as possible without hooking up on the bottom. Once I get a fish on I move as far and as quickly as possible to the rocks on the left so I can pull the fish out of the fast water and play him in the slow backwater of the eddy. If there is more than one fisherman on the rocks we rotate our casts about one minute apart and keep out of each other's way and still catch fish without disturbing our partner.

My favorite lure for fishing the rocks is a small Spin-N-Glo. Use a three-way, in-line swivel and attach a pencil lead weight about 30 inches above the Spin-N-Glo. Adjust the size of the weight depending on the size line you are using and the amount of current you are fishing in.

An alternate setup is to use a split-shot sinker tied three 3 feet above a single egg or flesh fly. Again, cast out into the current as far as you can and let the fly drift into the back eddy. When the fly swings into the slow water you will get a hookup if the fish are there and willing. Try a few casts with the same amount of line out and then shorten your cast 4 feet and try again. Keep decreasing the length of your cast until you find the fish. Once you get into the hole it has been my experience that you will have repeated takers.

When fishing from the rocks you will catch a mixed bag of grayling, Dollies, and rainbow. But no matter the species of fish you catch and release, you will always catch and keep a pleasant memory.

Margaret's Kenai King

Margaret's rod tip drops quickly and she shouts, "Oh, oh, oh, fish on!" It's obvious there is no king on the other end, but the first fish nevertheless. In less than a minute the team of Don, the guide, and Margaret boat a small Dolly.

No sooner is the Tad Poly back in the water than the deafening silence is broken. Margaret's reel spool begins turning backward. Line comes off in 20 and 30-yard spurts in rapid succession. The yet unseen king pauses in underwater flight, giving Margaret a moment to catch her breath and recapture some of the line.

A new plan to jettison the Tad Poly is put into play by the king. Retreat did not work. Now attack is attempted by charging directly for the boat faster than Margaret can reel. Only the depth of the water and pressure of the current against the line, keeping it tight, preserves the battle. The king stops opposite the boat in water too deep for a sighting. Margaret has not seen the fish yet. She again feels the pull of the living log as the line tightens. The rest stop for the king was near the bottom. Now using the water from the bottom to the surface for momentum, a 65-pound king salmon bursts into full view 12 feet from the boat. Elements of surprise and fear almost work to free the fish.

In desperation, Margaret tries to give the rod to me. I won't touch it. I wouldn't dare touch the rod, and run the risk of losing the fish. I can imagine the humiliation I would be required to suffer if I was viewed to be responsible for the loss if it got away. Don enjoys verbally assisting his client, but declines to participate beyond a coaching spectator. Three more high-flying attempts to dislodge the hook and flee seem to sap the king's remaining strength.

At that very moment Margaret, too, is ready to surrender. Only the encouragement from the fans keeps her hands on the rod and her heart in the battle. Fifteen more minutes of prolonged pulling, working against the current, brings the king close enough for the net. Don demonstrates his skill at landing big fish with one pass of the net for the final capture of the big Kenai king.

Margaret begins to rub aching muscles and her normal breathing returns. I begin to sulk and nurse a sore ego. She has outfished me. The first, the most, and the biggest.

Following the instructions of the guide, in keeping with the law, she puts up her rod. Her daily bag limit filled, now her fishing trip becomes a boat ride. I mutter something about now that everyone else is out of the way, maybe I can fish. She offers only encouragement. Not once does she rub it in.

Two turns above the takeout point I hit pay dirt. The Tad Polly produces my only hit of the day. It'as a good hit and hold. Soon my fishing also becomes a boat ride. The landing becomes a healing salve to my wounded ego. With both fish on board, it is obvious that Margaret's is at least 15 pounds heavier than mine. Margaret's only mention of comparison is that mine is a little darker. Not smaller, not a lot smaller, only darker.

Margaret carries her king picture in her wallet beside our grandchildren's photos. She will show it with a little prompting. She has relived the landing of her fish many times, but never has she confessed to outfishing me.

Mackey Maulers and Dogs

Gary Chilcote, our pilot-guide, informs Lee Fisher, my fishing partner and me that the species of fish we intend to do battle with is "Chum salmon!"

"Chum salmon?" my mind asks. "Chum salmon! Call them by their real name. Dogs!" Dog salmon, I'm told, inherited their name from Alaska Natives who use the four other species of Pacific salmon for food, barter, or sale, and feed the chum to the dogs. Dogs are evil-looking salmon. Giant mouths with canine teeth give the appearance of a mad dog. The look is only superficial. They strike like an aged Saint Bernard on vacation and fight like a Mexican Chihuahua at siesta. The pigment on the skin adds a horrible appearance of pale pink with several rows of calico stripes. No other Alaska migratory fish can match it for ugliness.

Lee, using a lure of his own making he calls a Mackey Mauler, works his lure about 12 inches under the surface. About 20 feet from shore a small wave follows the Mauler from a distance of 3 feet. Underneath the wave is undoubtedly a fish. With only 10 feet of line still out, the wave suddenly disappears and the single hook on the Mackey Mauler comes up empty.

Lee casts again. We observe a moving mound of water, the telltale sign of attack. Like a ballistic missile at hypersonic speed the fish moves as if in retaliation for missing on the first pass. Lee is also determined there will be no near miss. Neither fish nor angler is disappointed. The fish ensures a direct hit, striking with perfect accuracy.

Suddenly, breaking water, burst what I thought to be a small, but active, king. Now the salmon's motives change. Seconds before, the lure had been the object of pursuit and capture, and it's now escape and avoid. This change of heart creates a fighting fish on parity with any I've witnessed. The power of the strike would have pulled the rod from Fisher's fingers had he not been fully prepared.

What I thought, on first impression, to be a king has now changed my mind. Only a silver is out of the water like this fish. Adding evidence to my new thought is the bright silver light bouncing off his sides each time he decides to walk on water. Silvers exhibit tricks unknown to other salmon. This fish uses them all. First he tries to escape by running away. When this doesn't produce the desired result, he tries jumping, adding a few midair twists and turns. Reversing instantly from a 30 yard reel-ruining run, he directs his attack on the fisherman. The quick turnaround gives the fish the advantage of surprise. Now, moving right for Lee, in directly the opposite direction of seconds before, the fish takes charge. With slack in the line, he tries desperately to throw the hook. Ten feet from shore he comes out of the water shaking his head in a negative motion and spits the hook at Lee's feet. Now free of all containment, he swims away wiser for the experience. Lee, too, has been to school. The last 10 minutes have taught him a few lessons on landing lunkers.

Fired by the battle, Fisher makes another cast. As if in a rerun, the last strike repeats. The battle continues exactly as before with only one variation. This time the quick turnaround is anticipated and planned for. The fish never gets ahead and ends up on the beach being photographed for Lee to carry in his wallet.

While photographing the catch, we make a discovery. It is neither king nor silver. The instigator of all this action is a dog—I mean chum salmon. Bright silver body without even a trace of calico stripes. No fang-like teeth. Just a beautiful fish. Full of energy and fight. Having not seen chums fresh from the ocean, I had surmised the creatures were born ugly.

I suspect future judgement of fish will be tempered by my experience in western Alaska, in early June, on a secret fishing river, close to salt water.

Dream Trip

Bill Johnston from Omaha, Nebraska and I met at Anchorage International Airport where our trip to fish Iliamna began. Bill had won Alaska Outdoors magazine's Alaska Dream Trip Contest, the prize being a fishing trip to Alaska, fishing for a week with the magazine's editor. Almost before we had time to shake hands we were whisked to Era's flight to Iliamna.

On our arrival at Iliamna, Dean Spear, our guide for the week, met us when the plane landed. We were shown our rooms and made familiar with the rest of the lodge. Dean then discussed the plan for the week, beginning that afternoon on the Newhalen River . The Newhalen is just a short drive from the lodge, and is famous for rainbow trout in the 10- to 15-pound range.

I held the hot rod for the afternoon and caught the rainbow of the day—an 8-pounder on an egg fly. Bill gave me a go for it, but couldn't seem to get past the 7-pound mark. He would hook up, but for some reason he just couldn't land them.

Bill enjoyed the flight to, and the fishing at, the lodge's Ugashik Narrows camp. The water at Ugashik was so clear, he could see huge char holding behind the spawning sockeye, awaiting a meal of salmon eggs. Bill caught char, one after another, ranging in size from 3 to 6 pounds. Often everyone fishing had a hookup at the same time. Not only char, but Ugashik-Narrows-size arctic grayling and silver salmon added to the excitement.

The last day was perhaps the highlight of the week. Chief pilot Mark Keen flew us, one at a time, in his wheel-equipped Supercub bush plane. By using this plane and his knowledge of the area, we were able to fish streams we felt had never been fished.

Late in the afternoon Bill released a silver back to the river to spawn. Turning, he said with a grin, "A fella can get down-right tired fishing in Alaska." Bill rubbed his arms, sore from catching so many big fish. It looked like he was about to give up, and stop fishing for the day. No way. He took a deep breath, and waded into the river to make his next cast. He stood there, more slowly retrieving his lure now, staring off at the mountains and the sun retreating behind them. He was all fished out. Alaska had won. She had furnished more fishing than the angler could take. Bill put away his rod and surrendered to his surroundings.

We flew back to the lodge tired and happy, enjoying the mountains, and the wildlife below. Fall colors were creeping across the tundra. Bull moose sported huge white antlers, reflecting light, and gave away their location. Caribou were abundant. We spotted brown bear walking beaches, or standing in rivers fishing. Bill was in awe of the scenery, the fishing, and the lodge.

Bill Johnston from Omaha, Nebraska is glad he took his dream trip to the Iliamna country. Perhaps next time it will be your dream trip. And, why not? Someone's going to do it. Why not you?

Angler's Telegraph

Sportfishing is Alaska's number one sport and outdoor recreation activity. More people participate in fishing than in all other Alaska leisure activities combined. Alaskans spend their vacations, holidays, days off, and time before and after work in pursuit of fish. A large percentage of visitors to the Great Land spend their time with rod in hand, and millions yet to visit dream of fishing Alaska.

Alaska is a land of unlimited fishing opportunities, but it is almost impossible to get your arms around the entire Alaska angling possibilities in one lifetime. For more than four decades I've fished the state, both for pleasure and as my vocation, and I have only approached the potential.

Different from most other states where fishermen are required to go to the fish, Alaska is unique—the fish come to the angler. Each season five different species of Pacific salmon migrate to their natal streams, bringing other varieties with them. Following the salmon, these beggars are seeking an easy meal, mostly of salmon eggs. This phenomenon provides fish-hatchery-like populations for anglers to throw a line to.

The precise time of the run's return to a given watershed cannot be predicted, but it will be within a few days of its anticipated occurrence. The miracle of returning fish is almost exceeded by the marvel of how quickly the word spreads to waiting anglers. A whispered, "Reds are in the Russian," is heard seemingly simultaneously by thousands of waiting sportsmen. One day the stream is void of anglers—and fish—and the next morning the banks are lined with the hopeful. Every area along the road system in the state enjoys the same kind of angler's telegraph. Gas stations, restaurants, gift stores, and tackle shops know within an hour when the first few fish are taken from any roadside water.

If an angler is on the stream concurrent with the spawning run, it is almost impossible to not catch fish, even if only basic fishing techniques are employed. More important than all the how-to, where-to books and guides written, information obtained from local sources are the most reliable. Anglers can get more real angling assistance from filling station attendants, store clerks, and waitresses, than from a library of written material and a month of reading. Books may predict the run within a week, but the guy pumping gas or the gal serving breakfast is the best source for timely and helpful information about the run. Their source—angler's telegraph.

Copper River Dip Net

We drove to Chitna to witness Alaska residents taking red salmon with long-handled dip nets. The Copper River's water near Chitna is filled with glacial silt. Thousands upon thousands of returning red salmon run the river to their natal clear-water stream entering the silty Copper. The State allows residents to subsistence-fish using dip nets.

Experienced dip-net fishermen develop a technique to capture and preserve their catch. Most purchase a dip net with a 10- or 12-foot handle. By using hose clamps and duct tape, they attach an additional 10-foot extension to the existing handle. To this they add, again with hose clamps and duct tape, a crutch. The crutch gives the user a handle to manipulate the net in deep, swift river water. Most subsistence fishermen wear neoprene chest waders.

Fishing is accomplished by holding on to the crutch handle and throwing the net end of the apparatus upstream and out into the current. By twisting the crutch handle, the user is able to keep the net vertical as it drifts downriver with the water flow. Due to the murky water, the fish cannot be seen and the action is strictly guessing. When the vertically held net drifts as far downriver as possible, its user turns the crutch handle. Turning the handle closes the horizontal net and traps any netted fish.

We witnessed a family of four generations filling their freezer for the winter—literally. They brought a chest-type freezer mounted on a utility trailer and energized by a portable generator. Four family members took turns with two nets. As each fisherman got tired and cold, he would rotate with one of the others. When a red salmon was taken in the net, one of several skilled women or teenagers would quickly and skillfully dispatch the fish, fillet it, and wrap it for the freezer. We arrived in the middle of the afternoon and their 20-cubic-foot freezer was nearly full. The young man I visited told me they came every year, and one day's fishing supplied their extended family with all the fish they required for one year.

Watching this family work as a team in harvesting one of Alaska's bounties was an interesting experience. Although taking an unseen salmon from muddy water with a net didn't excite either the angler or the spectator like a tail-walking red on a rod, it was fun to observe. I trust their fishing stories over Sunday dinner are not too different from those of fishermen who subsist with rod and reel.

Deshka Dardevle

My first fly-in fishing trip in Alaska was to the Deshka River in 1959 during silver salmon season. We fished all evening and had the mouth of the river to ourselves. Back then, Bob Farmer was a teenager tending his father's boat rental business a mile or so up from where the Deshka meets the Big Susitna. We were his only customers of the afternoon, renting a 12-foot aluminum car-top boat with a 10-horsepower outboard motor.

Our party of three inexperienced anglers, using minimum fishing gear borrowed from a neighbor, and lacking a knowledge of the river, almost went home skunked. At first we thought there weren't any silvers although Bob Farmer said a run of fresh fish had just entered the river's mouth. Occasionally we saw a jumper or two, but none were interested in our meager offerings. They ignored everything we threw at them. Admittedly, we didn't know what we were doing and we didn't have a great variety of terminal tackle.

About the time we were ready to give up I discovered an old, experienced-looking florescent Dardevle in the bottom of our borrowed tackle box. As a last resort, I attached it to my line and made a hope cast. No sooner than the lure began its wiggle-waggle a fresh silver hit like it was mad at everyone in the boat and at Bob Farmer upstream in his dad's tent camp. With little skill and a great amount of luck, I got the fish close enough to the boat for my fishing buddy, Ron, to net my catch.

Catching of the prime silver prompted us to continue fishing, where just minutes before we were ready to give up and go home skunked. We each in turn took another cast, my turn being last. As Ron and Ted dragged their lures through the murky water, my lure was tossed in the direction opposite from their casts. Again, to my surprise and delight, another silver rallied to the call and tried to take my lure down the Big Su. My partners quickly brought their lines in and assisted me in landing my second silver.

And so it went for the third, fourth, and fifth fish. We now had five fish in the boat, my legal limit. I quit fishing and Ron took my rod. Like my five casts with the fluorescent Dardevle, Ron was soon playing and landing five silvers. At first, Ted had continued fishing but he quickly put his rod away and became the designated net man.

With the boating of Ron's legal limit, Ted and Ron traded rod for net and Ted took his turn with the fluorescent Dardevle. Just as the 10 casts before had produced 10 strikes, the next five casts did likewise and Ted soon had his limit of fish in the bottom of the boat.

After cleaning the fish and returning our boat to the Farmers, we headed back to Anchorage's Lake Hood floatplane base. While Ron and Ted tied up the plane, I put the gear away. I couldn't find the fluorescent Dardevle and I asked them about it. They hadn't seen it. They didn't know what happened to it. They said I must have dropped it, or lost it, or something.

I learned later that the next day, while I worked, Ted and Ron returned to the Deshka and caught 10 silvers on 10 casts using an old fluorescent Dardevle.

Fish Fry

My friend Jerry, knowing he was going to Dillingham at the height of the commercial red salmon season, invited a rather large group of friends to a fish-fry. He left the impression with the group that he was going fishing and would supply the fish. He didn't mention, however, that he was going commercial fishing with a commercial fisherman for a day. His friends, convinced that he was fishing with a fly rod, were impressed with his confident manner.

As scheduled, a few days before the planned fish fry, Jerry caught the jet from Anchorage to Dillingham. His commercial fishing buddy intended to pick him up and they'd go to his boat and fish for an open period. Jerry'd then dash back to the airport, jet home, and be there a day ahead of his ego-building fish fry. Only one problem, storms and tide had kept his commercial fishing partner stranded in a safe cove some miles from Dillingham. He had managed a message that he couldn't make it and suggested Jerry get back on the plane and go home.

During the flight, Jerry contemplated what he was to do. He couldn't cancel the fish fry, and if he held the fish fry with store-bought fish, he sure couldn't let his friends know. They'd laugh him out of town. What was he to do?

Somewhere in flight he got an idea that involved me and that's the reason I got the telephone call. "Hi Evan, why don't we go down to the Russian River and catch some reds?" he asked.

Knowing the reds hadn't arrived yet prompted me to decline his suggestion. "Maybe another time" I said.

"No" said Jerry. "It's got to be tomorrow."

"Why tomorrow?" I asked.

And then Jerry told me his missed-the-fish tale. So we decided to give it a try and we headed for the Russian in my motor home. Arriving at the Russian River Campground around midnight, we were met by the taker of the tolls and given the information that the reds, "just ain't quite in yet." Since we were already there, we decided to stay and see what we could find when it got light.

I have a favorite hole on the upper Russian and we headed there when morning came over the mountains. Jerry also had a pet spot, which I found out was around the corner above mine. I stopped where I'd had good luck in the past and Jerry went on upriver as I waded to the other side of the Russian and found my spot. Jerry disappeared out of sight.

Donning polaroid glasses, I searched the pool where I wanted to fish and found three reds resting in the current. They were either hungry or foolish as one by one they nipped at my Russian River fly and I moved them out of the hole and downriver to slack water where I could complete the landing. Three times I tried and each time a red responded, and then the hole was empty. No more fish. But I had my limit, so I quit and waded back to the trail and waited for Jerry's return.

About an hour later the dejected angler came dragging his feet down the trail. "Not even a bite," Jerry said. "Not one fish in my hole. How'd you do?"

When he saw my three reds he just about exploded with excitement. He'd told me earlier, he needed at least three fish, and there they were, three nice reds, cleaned and ready for Jerry's fish fry.

I don't know what Jerry told his friends, or if he mentioned anything about where the fish for the fry came from. I do know, however, that I've talked to some of the folks who fried the fish with Jerry, and they think he's the best fly-fisherman in Alaska. And why shouldn't they, they ask, "He had a fresh fish fry before anyone else had even caught a fish."

Floating and Fishing
with Feathers

It is difficult to conceive of arriving at the age of accountability without a memory of at last one fish fracturing the surface of some aqueous setting. Then came one Rick Nita from Los Angeles, California confessing the absence of fishing in his life. He admitted to a feeling of remorse and a yearning to repent. Rick picked Alaska as the place, opted for a float trip, selected rainbow as the game, mid-September as the date, feathers as the weapon.

He arrived in Anchorage with a borrowed rod and reel and not knowing if a tippet was a part of the gear, good to eat, or some kind of snare. He relied on the local tackle store to "fix him up," and was treated kindly.

With mosquito dope in his pocket, new flies tucked in his new vest, and armed with his adopted rod and reel, he arrived at the Anchorage airport for the flight to Iliamna. Here Rick met his companions: four members of the Orange County California Fly-Fishing Club, freelance outdoor writer Hank Bottemiller and his son Dave, and from Boston, Mike Ableson.

His apprehension of being a complete novice among experts drifted away with each introduction and handshake. Each man reassured him and committed to help Rick get started off right without embarrassment. He was taught a few basic knots, how to get the line out with a couple of false casts, and the ease of the double haul for distance.

The rainbow he landed on his first cast will not register in any record book. The bow didn't even make the frying pan. Rick began his catch-and-release career on his original catch. Any fears Rick might have had that this would be his only fish were erased on the next cast. Another rainbow slammed the former covering of birds and immediately showed its belly to the sun. It goes without saying that Rick was endowed with beginner's luck. Some days he caught more than 80 rainbows, plus grayling, char, chum, king, and silver salmon.

Well, he almost caught a silver. On the next-to-last day of the float trip, casting into a deep hole, Rick let out a Southern-California-Japanese-American-first-time-fishing warhoop as a silver salmon broke water and headed for the ocean. At the same time, Dave Bottemiller, Rick's fishing companion, set the hook on his fifth silver of the afternoon. Rick played it perfect, letting the salmon do most of the work. The fish made one final run and beached itself, resulting in shouts of praise and pats on his back for Rick's first silver salmon.

Dave, the more experienced fisherman, just smiled. He knew something Rick didn't. When the flip-flopping slowed down and the congratulations subsided, it was discovered that two lines ran to the fish. Rick's and Dave's. They had both been fishing the same pool. The fish had hit Dave's lure and tangled with Rick's line. Dave allowed Rick to land the fish and enjoy the thrill of landing a powerful silver. For those who keep track of such things, as far as silver salmon are concerned, the score is really Dave, five—Rick, zero.

It seemed the final morning came before the week began. Breaking camp for the last time. Deflating the rafts. The group picture for the scrapbook, and the concluding cast as the Cessna 206 taxied in. The flight to Anchorage and beyond to home.

Back in California, Rick will tell you a float trip is a kick-back, easy-living type of experience. It is unhurried, almost without schedule. Body and soul relax. The tired and hurried world of everyday living stays with the drop-off plane. After a week's fishing a remote Alaska river, life never returns with the same consuming intensity.

Friendships are established with the guides and other fishermen. Ten o'clock sunsets, 5 a.m. sunrises, midnight fireside chats, wildlife, camp at the bend of the river, beaver tail slap, remoteness of the area, absence of other people, and of course, fishing—that's a float trip.

A float trip is remote. A float trip is standing in crystal-clear water, where perhaps no other living person has stood, drifting a fly past a grayling that has never seen anything artificial, breaking the deafening silence with shouts of excitement where no human has ever spoken. That's fishing with feathers on a float trip.

Grand Slam Salmon

Jerry Pippen, of Rainbow Bay Resort, and I were trying to do something no one had ever done, catch all five species of Pacific salmon in on day.

"There they are!" A deep hole contained about 20 kings.

"Is that bar upstream on the right long enough to get in and out of?"

"I think it'll be okay."

Master bush pilot Pippen picked his spot for touchdown and set the Piper Cub up for landing. The huge tundra tires caught the tops of grass and undergrowth and the bush plane settled onto the improvised landing field. Our sandbar airport was, in reality, one of the islands forming the Alagnak River braids. Two hundred yards below the island two other branches of the braids joined into a deep water run where kings lay.

"They're there alright," Jerry said. "Now all we got to do is catch one. Fish on!"

"Fish off," Jerry responded. "It was a rainbow." Jerry got a taker on every cast. "Another rainbow," Jerry complained. "Where's the king?" he muttered as he released a 22-inch 'bow.

"Hey, Jerry. How many clients do you have who'd complain about this kind of rainbow fishing?"

Jerry's line went tight as his experienced reflexes automatically set the hook on what he instinctively knew was a big fish. "Here's what we came for!" he shouted. "All we got to do now is get him in and take his picture."

Pippen seldom missed with a well-hooked fish and the king's fight was stalled long enough for a stand-up bow for my camera. Almost concurrent with the release, Jerry and I turned toward the airplane for the flight to the coast.

Jerry's intended stopover for two more species was a short stretch of clear, fresh water emptying into Lower Cook Inlet. Confirming the direction of the prevailing winds, Jerry turned the Cub for a short downwind, then final, a short rollout landing on the gravel beach, and finally taxied to a stop 20 feet from the fishing hole.

The first cast produced a pink and the second fish toward a grand slam. I recorded the event on film. With the release, Jerry moved upriver hoping for a chum. Several large chum salmon were swimming in a clear pool at the foot of a small waterfall.

"Like shooting fish in a barrel," quipped the confident fisherman as he cast into a group of chum salmon. A fish sighted the lure and attacked. Jerry set the hook. The fight lasted only long enough to make it interesting and the third member of Pippen's grand slam was soon held for the recording eye of my camera.

"We got three. Let's go to the lodge and catch a sockeye while the boys gas up the plane. We can then go on up the inlet for a silver."

On landing, Jerry and I mounted the four-wheeler and headed for a bay on Lake Iliamna. "Gas her up and we'll be right back," instructed Jerry. "It won't take long to land a sockeye."

Jerry was right. Almost before I could get my camera adjusted for the late afternoon sun, Jerry landed and released the fourth species of his grand slam. "Number four is down. Silver coming up!"

The sun was completing its setting at 11:30 when the red and white airplane turned final approach. "We'll have to be real lucky. I hope the fish are here and they will take my lure," Jerry commented to no one as he hurried toward the hole. "Hope we're lucky," thinking out loud as he cast across the hole.

The fish were there and they took his lure. Silvers go airborne as soon as they feel the bite of the hook and pressure of line restraining their movement and Jerry's grand slam silver was no exception. In the failing light, Jerry and I saw the tail-dancing silver waltz across the hole.

It appeared that Jerry's goal would soon be realized and the fish would be subdued. I, outfitting my camera with a flash attachment, anxiously awaited the right moment to snap the photo. In my mind I even prepared words of congratulation for Jerry.

The fish twisted and became entangled in the line and Jerry slowly inched the concluding element of his quest toward shore. He bent and reached for the fish and lifted the rod tip to bring it closer. The fish rolled with the tension on the line, became untangled, and, leaving a spray of mud and water, darted away. Instinctively, Jerry quickly raised his rod tip to reset the pressure. In the darkness, Jerry had not observed his line was caught on the reel handle. As the line tightened, the inevitable occurred, with the line snapping and the fish escaping.

Where victory had been only inches away, Jerry silently stood, stunned by fate's flustering feat. The fish, as if to add insult to injury, boomeranged and bounced from one side of the hole to the other. Time and time again it stood on its tail, and, with the lure still in its mouth, shook its head at the disenchanted Alaskans. Finally, having scolded them into an admission of defeat, it made one final leap and disappeared forever from their sight.

Jerry looked at his watch. In the darkness he could hardly make out the numbers. Finally his eyes focused. Four minutes past midnight. Time had run out.

Grand Slam Salmon 2

Yes, there is a time, most years at least, when there are a few of all five species of Pacific Salmon in the Goodnews River," Mike Gorton responded to my question.

"Do you think, if I came out, I could catch at least one of each species on a fly rod in one day—a salmon grand slam?" I asked.

"I do. This would be a perfect year. It's an even-numbered year and the pinks will be in," Mike replied. "Bring your fly rod the last week in July. We can do it. We'll make it happen."

An so the stage was set. The same stage I had been on many times in the past ten years. The lodge or guide thought we could do it, and then something conspired to prevent the salmon grand slam. Like two years ago when I took the three most difficult ones in the first hour of fishing in Kachemak Bay. First it was a feeder king, and then a red, and finally, a silver. Three times the gear went out and each time it came back with a different species.

The guide, Steve Novokavich of Cruiser Five Charters was as delighted as I was. The only thing left was a pink and a chum, and it was a pink year again—an even-numbered year. Steve knew a place where we could beach his boat, let me off, anchor his boat out, and come to shore in his dinghy. We'd then hike a mile or so up a clear-water stream to a hole beneath a waterfall where taking a pink and a chum would be, as Steve said, "like shooting fish in a barrel."

The hole was as Steve described. I couldn't miss. The hole was loaded with fish. It was the ideal setup. It was the ideal setup for a large, mean-looking and-acting black bear as well.

No sooner had I started to get my rod ready, then he came charging into the hole and I had to leave. I didn't want a mad, hungry black bear on the end of my line or in my face. We waited, hoping he'd fill up and leave, but the tide changed before he left and we had to give up the grand slam challenge and return to the boat.

This year's setup was different. I'd have a guide, a boat, and 240 miles of heaven-created fly-fishing water to pursue the challenge. I was sure it'd be good news on the Goodnews River.

When I arrived at Goodnews River Lodge I was greeted by a group of guides who had drawn straws to see who would be first to try the Grand Slam Salmon Challenge with me, and if we failed on the first try, who'd be in line for the next day's attempt.

About the time I was ready to go for it, I learned that the rules had been changed by the Department of Fish and Game and king season closed the day before my arrival. The only way I could get a Grand Slam Salmon was to catch the king incidentally while fishing for other species. I couldn't target a king. I was ready to give up when the guide suggested we just go fishing and see what happened. And so we did.

Every day I fished I took three or four species, and always a king. The river was full of kings and it was hard to keep them off my line. A king on a light fly rod is hard work and it interfered with other fishing.

Then came guide Dave Ward's day. He was sure we could get the species we had been denied earlier and we'd just have to see what'd happen on a king. I wasn't too hopeful. I'd been disappointed too many times before.

Dave started me out on the main river near salt water as the tide was coming in. He said that maybe an early silver would come with the tide. On the first cast a weak-kneed chum struck and succumbed quickly to my urging to shore. Then, a few casts later, a pink gave up. Following the pink a huge, fresh, sea-run silver tried to separate me from my fly—and it was successful. In my excitement to land the fish I allowed the line to wrap around my little finger just as the silver was returning to salt water. My pride and my pinky suffered about the same. Both damaged, but not fatal.

A few casts later another, but smaller silver took the fly and scooted under a submerged log, lodging the line tight and preventing a fair fight. Dave quickly responded and freed the line before the fish could work it to the breaking point. More by good luck than good management the little silver was soon brought to hand and released.

Dave directed me to the boat suggesting that we go upriver and try for a sockeye, and if successful we'd just go fishing and see what'd happen. On the way to the reds, Dave pulled into a hole where two branches of the Goodnews come together. There was a bunch of fish finning, including a few reds.

"Let's try here for a bit. Maybe we won't have to go upriver," Dave said as he threw out the anchor. "I think maybe the whole grand slam may be in this hole," Dave said, more to himself than to me.

I got a few hits, but nothing solid. Then I felt a fish move the fly and Dave exploded with "Set the hook, set the hook!" as my line started playing off the screaming reel. "It's got to be a king. Not too big, but no chum ever ran like that," Dave cried.

After a few minutes of tug-of-war the yet unseen fish turned upriver and returned to the quiet water where he first took the bait. The long first run and fight back to the hole had exhausted the fish and as he slipped closer to the boat, I knew I had a king if I'd keep my fingers out of the way.

"Bring him in quick," Dave said. "We don't want to tire him too much. Let's bring him in now and let him go and do his thing." And with that, Dave reached over the gunnel, slipped his right hand around the fish's tail and removed the barbless hook out of the king's mouth with the other hand.

I didn't even get a chance to contemplate what had happened before Dave was telling me to sit down in the boat. "We're heading for the sockeye hole. This is the day you get your grand slam."

About 30 minutes later Dave got the boat parked and was leading me to his sockeye hole. I sensed Dave's excitement which increased my own. Dave, holding his thumb and index finger close together with only a sliver of light between said, "I can almost guarantee your Grand Slam."

I thought to myself, "I've been here many times before."

Dave didn't need to cross his fingers or hold them apart.

Five minutes after our arrival, an acrobatic red was fished out of the hole, brought to shore, and released. I had my grand slam. Dave was jumping up and down with joy. I was numb. I just then was beginning to realize my quest was over. I'd taken the grand slam salmon on a fly rod! Now that it was over, what's left? But now I realized it wasn't the catching I wanted as much as chasing the challenge.

What's left? I guess It'll be a sockeye on a deer hair mouse.

Listen to the Guide

One Kodiak river I never tire of fishing is the Karluk. On my first trip to Karluk it was during the short boat ride from the airport to the lodge that I began receiving my Karluk River education. The guide explained that the fish come in on the tide. It is best to start fishing at the mouth just as the tide starts moving. Follow the fish as they move upriver into the lagoon. Once high water is reached, the fishing will stop. There will be no more fish at the mouth until the next tide. The fish will move upriver into the holes and it will be hot up there when it's not any good down at the mouth. By the time the fish move through the upper holes and on upriver, it's time to go back and try the mouth again. Somewhere in between there'll be time for three meals and sleep.

My excitement of fishing the Karluk was short-lived when I met Paul, one of the lodge's guests. "How's the fishing?" I asked.

"Not too good. It's the same here as at the lodge where I was last year. I had a good time but the fishing was not what it was cracked up to be. I just don't think Alaska fishing is all that great. My guide thinks I'll do better at the mouth. He says the kings will be coming in on the tide. I hope it's not just another guide story."

The guide shouted, "Fish on!" as Paul hooked up on his first cast. The fish started upriver and then turned down and headed for the open sea. The guide assumed his role and began to counsel Paul. "Keep the tip up, let the rod do the work."

The fish took line out at about 10 yards a second. Paul turned his drag tighter and the guide told him to leave it alone. "It's set right. Don't tighten the drag, move along the beach with the fish."

As if he didn't hear, Paul planted his feet firmly on shore and tightened the drag. The rod tip dropped until it was pointed directly at the running fish. The line continued to play off the reel as Paul leaned back and held on. The telltale rifle-shot-like sound of breaking line signaled the end of the fight as Paul almost fell over backward when the forward pull quit abruptly.

The guide discovered that Paul's reel was completely worn out. All the gears were gone. "It's a new reel," Paul exclaimed, "It can't be broken already."

The guide tried to explain. "Paul, you're using a very heavy line. The drag is set way too tight. These are big strong fish right from the ocean, and you need to follow them downriver and out of swift water." The guide loaned Paul another outfit brought along for just such an emergency.

Inasmuch as Paul had hooked up on his first cast he was now the expert and would not listen to the guide. He was wearing chest waders and insisted on standing in water over his waist, even if it meant wading into the hole and casting beyond the fish. As the tide advanced, the guide moved me and two other guests up the lagoon to the rock pile. Paul insisted on fishing where he had earlier hooked the fish. We soon limited out and began fishing for sport. Paul continued to ignore the guide and came up empty.

When the tide peaked, the fishing quit. The fish moved on up the lagoon out of reach. We headed for the lodge and dinner. Paul remained to fish the outgoing tide where he stayed until dark. He reported that he didn't even get a bite. He had tenacity, but he didn't have enough sense to listen to the guide.

The next two days were repeats of the first afternoon. Up-river and down everyone caught fish. Sockeyes, kings, Dollies, and rainbows. Everyone except Paul. Finally in frustration the guide waded out to where Paul was standing.

"Paul, you've got to listen to me. You're standing right where the fish are moving through. You fish at the wrong time, in the wrong place, use the wrong lure, and the wrong approach. If you want to catch fish, you've got to listen to me."

Paul's response was, "I'll try a few more casts here and then move on up." With that, the guide gave up on Paul.

Guides tell me there are guys like Paul on almost every trip. They think they know more than the guide and keep fishing "a better way." Guides take personal pride in seeing their clients catch fish. When they don't, it's almost a personal affront. There is competition among guides at every fishing lodge. They add up the score of the day's catch with each other. They don't like it if someone doesn't catch fish. They'll break their backs to make sure their client has the best possible chance to land what he paid money for.

Alaska is a fish-rich state. No one need ever come up empty fishing its waters. Most anglers have enough brains to look around and follow other successful fishermen when they themselves are not doing well. Almost everyone will share bait ideas or techniques with others who are willing to listen.

I hope anyone Paul tells "the fishing in Alaska is not what it's cracked up to be," knows better. I wish Paul would return to the Karluk. Next time, Paul, listen to your guide and you'll catch fish until you wish you hadn't listened.

The First Catch and Release

Mt. McKinley's 20,320-foot summit guards the Interior's southern flank and the Brooks Range stands watch to the north. East is the Yukon border and the west converges to the Bering Sea. Most of the country is covered with low, rolling hills. Braided rivers cross the country on their way to the sea. The great rivers of the gold rush: Yukon, Tanana, Porcupine, Koyukuk, and others, still serve as much of the Interior's only highways.

Interior's summer is a paradox—short in number of days, but long in hours of daylight per day. Almost 24 hours of light bless anglers who want to fish 'round the clock. This is the place to take off your watch and without thought of time, fish when you want.

Unless a timepiece is consulted, far north adventurers cannot tell the time of day. While fishing the Interior, anglers may fish until midnight under a brilliant sun. The sun will set slowly and turn pink or red behind northern hills, only to hesitate, and begin its upward climb as a stunning sunrise.

What rainbow trout are to Western Alaska, pike, grayling, and sheefish are to the Interior. Northern pike weighing up to 30 pounds and more may be taken. In season, some area lakes and streams will be choked with migrating grayling. Sheefish haunt the Yukon River and its tributaries, the lower Chena River, and Minto Flats streams. Rainbow, not indigenous to the area, have been planted in many lakes along the road system.

Vermont colors pale when compared to an Interior fall. Although short, the period between long sunny summer days and freeze-up is an outstanding display of Mother Nature's colors. Every color in God's paint pot is on parade in a procession of public performances that brings goose bumps to all but the most jaded observer. Across the tundra and through the trees and brush, travelers are treated to exhibitions of tincture from octopus black to celestial white, from blazing blue to flaming red to scorching yellow. If there was ever a time and place for an artist to witness every imaginable hue and color, Interior in the fall meets the exact criteria.

While waiting for our ride at the end of an Interior fall outing, we gathered bits and pieces of tundra color. Three of us, during the doldrums of waiting, fashioned an arctic scavenger hunt. We crossed and crisscrossed the tundra and retrieved morsels of color to photograph for an outstanding representation of the area's coloring. After an hour of searching, we returned to camp and assembled a composition almost impossible to paint. We marveled at the variety of hue, tone, tint, tinge, and density. The resulting photograph is one of my favorites.

Angling the Interior is fishing in a country unpopulated and in waters truly unpolluted. One of my choicest Alaska outings was fishing the far north with a Native Alaskan guide. We were on the Fish River and its tributaries. My guide had learned the river from his grandparents who learned from their grandparents; yet his skill with a fly rod and spinning rod were as modern as tomorrow. We were fishing a little "southeast of Nome," on a river named Fish, in country like all Alaska used to be, but will never be again.

Paul, my guide, passed on to me the ancient Eskimo catch and release custom he learned from his grandmother who learned it from her grandmother and so on back to the beginning. Ancient Eskimo fishermen returned the first fish they caught, believing it would tell the other fish how well he was treated and the others would come to find out for themselves.

My fishing partner and I decided that if it worked by releasing the first fish, we would find out what would happen if we released all the fish we caught. The results were so outstanding that we can now write a new chapter in the book on reasons for catch and release. Turn back the fish you capture and they will go and tell the rest how well they were treated and the others will seek you out.

Paul's grandmother, fishing with primitive instruments, may have known something we, in our age of boron and ball bearings, could learn about our angling pursuits. In Interior Alaska, on the Fish River, a little southeast of Nome, catch and release predated Trout Unlimited by centuries.

Humpies and Halibut

Jerry Pippen, Rainbow Bay's owner, invited me to join four Outside visitors and spend a day fishing for halibut and humpies. Jerry explained we would fish the morning high tide for humpies and the afternoon slack tide for halibut. We would rendezvous with guides and boats in the early morning and travel three miles to the humpies' creek.

Leaving the lodge in light planes under a star-filled sky, we arrived at the halibut camp at daylight. After a short boat ride we beached at a small stream entering the bay.

To the left and west of the stream was a steep alder-infested mountain. East of the creek was a 15-foot bluff overlooking the area. Bear trails ran along the edge of the bluff with exits at intervals allowing access to the water. At the far end of this small valley, between the mountain and the bluff, a stream 20 feet wide and 3 feet deep cascaded into a pool. The pool was created by a high bank on the beach between the bluff and the mountain. This pool was perhaps 100 feet long and 30 feet wide, and drinking-water-clear.

The pool was temporary home to a 10-feet-thick school of pink salmon. They were packed together so tight that if the center group of fish moved, the entire population went with it. The surface boiled with the backs and tails of migrating pink salmon fresh from the ocean.

The four Texans decided they must have died and gone to fisherman's heaven. They baited up with red pixies and began casting into the heart of the hole. They experienced no difficulty in hooking up with fish. Each had one on the first cast, the next cast, and the next.

After a couple of hours of nonstop fish fighting the group snacked on sandwiches beside a driftwood fire prepared by the guides. After lunch the group moved to the edges of the school and became more selective in their casts. There were fewer incidental hookups, less lost tackle, and greater enjoyment. The guys from Texas learned a fishing paradox: Too many fish can be just as boring as too few. They began their own contest, wagering high stakes on the outcome. Although none of the bets were taken seriously, they added to the excitement and fun of the afternoon.

Jerry found it almost impossible to get the crew away from the hole to fish for halibut. They complained of backs that ached, arms too weak to cast, and feet cold from standing in the water all day, but they would not give in and quit.

Finally they were coaxed to the boats for an hour's worth of bottom fishing. The light gear of the morning was traded for heavier halibut gear. Hoping for a halibut, fresh cut herring was applied to the terminal end of the line and dropped into the depths. When a fish was hooked the fishermen complained of being too tired to bring it up. They even passed the successful rod around the boat allowing everyone to share the work. A few halibut were caught, but the fishermen simply did not have their hearts in it. They were all fished out.

Finally Jerry put an end to their misery by stowing the gear away. Fatigue took over and each man propped his feet up on the rail, sat back in his chair, and contemplated what he must have considered to be the best fishing experience of his life.

Halibut on a Fly

Rocky Constant's client for the afternoon halibut tide was casting champion Steve Rajeff. His intent was to try and break the halibut 12-pound-line class world record.

Rocky put his party on the hole he was seeking and announced, "Let's go fishing. The tide is slack and the fish should be biting."

Steve made two false casts, then put the line 80 feet from the boat, letting the fly softly strike the water as if he were fishing for a brown trout back home. It took nearly a minute for the 900-grain shooting head to force the large herring-pattern fly to the bottom. Steve's experienced fingers, and his sixth sense, felt the line touch something solid and he began stripping it in. We on the surface could imagine the fly darting and twisting on the bottom, giving an appearance of a wounded herring to any deep sea onlooker.

No takers. Steve, unable to make a sale, brought his rig in for another try. The entire process of casting, stripping, and retrieving took five full minutes. Given 40 minutes of slack tide to fish, Steve would be able to cast a maximum of eight times for the world record he seeks.

Again feeling the bottom, the world casting champion and halibut line class challenger began to retrieve his line in a smooth stripping action. Then, the anticipated event occured. The line went tight and began moving away down the inlet.

"We've got a fish on," Steve said rather nonchalantly, not reflecting the excitement felt by the spectators.

"Set the hook. Give it a hard jerk. Pop it as hard as you can! Set the hook!" Rocky pleaded. He expected the hard-jarring-

line-snapping jerk associated with stiff halibut rods wearing 70-pound line. "Set the hook!"

"The hook's set," Steve assured. "I got him solid. This is only 12-pound line, remember, and a very limber rod."

"If he's very big, you won't be able to get him off the bottom. He won't even know he's hooked, no harder than you planted the hook," Rocky cautioned.

Steve's fly line was slowly retrieved, but there was very little pressure coming from the depths below the boat. Just a very steady pull.

"Sure doesn't pull very hard," Steve said. "Can't be very big."

"If it's a halibut, it's a small one. Must be a cod. Probably a cod." Rocky's voice contained an air of conviction, but at the same time he hoped he was wrong.

"I was wrong!" Rocky shouted as the dark shape of the fish was seen by all at the same time. "It's a halibut! It sure didn't seem like a halibut. You just barely pulled on him. There wasn't even a bow in your rod."

"I don't think he even knew he was hooked," Steve speculated. "I just coaxed him to the top with very little pressure. Figured if he decided to stay down, I was never going to pull him off the bottom with 12-pound test. As it worked out, I believe I could have landed him with 6-pound test line."

Thirty-three pounds, twelve ounces, the official scales read. "Thirty-three pounds, twelve ounces," the gathered crowd announced to each other as they read the scales dial. "Four ounces short of the world record. Four ounces short. Only four ounces. Probably lost four ounces coming in. Only four ounces!"

"As it worked out, I believe I could have landed him with 6-pound test line," Rocky remembered Steve's comment made on the way in. "I could have landed him with 6-pound test" "What's the world record on six-pound test?"

Hi-Ho Humpie

Have you noticed when you're fishing with a group of people, there is always one angler who just doesn't fit in with the group? I don't mean they have bad breath or a contrary personality. It's the fish they were catching or not catching. Like the time I was fishing in Southeast Alaska out of George Inlet Lodge. Everyone but one guy was catching halibut. The guy who didn't fit in was catching sand sharks. Every time his line went down, wearing the same bait as everyone else and fishing on the same side of the boat at the same depth, he came up with a sand shark.

Then there was the day I was fishing for silvers on the Little Camashack River. I couldn't miss. It was every cast a fighting, acrobatic silver. The next day when we returned, the person I was fishing with couldn't miss and I couldn't get a bite. We were fishing in the same hole, the same way, and exactly the same way as the day before, but if we had to eat our catch for lunch, I'd have gone hungry. To make matters worse, everyone else in the party was catching. I was the only one who couldn't buy a fish.

The same kind of a thing happened on the Little Susitna River fishing for silvers with guide Andy Couch, owner of FishTale River Guides. Besides myself, Andy's clients included my daughter-in-law, Rebecca, and my son Easten.

We started early since Andy said he'd like to be the first one on the Slide Hole that morning. No sooner had we arrived, than we began catching fish. Andy, the professional, outfished us, even though he was only trying to find the fish for us. He soon had three silvers in the cooler. I was next. This wasn't a catch and release day, this was meat-gathering-for-the-freezer angling. It wasn't long before Rebecca had three silvers on ice in Andy's cooler. Along the way we had taken and released a couple of pinks or chums. We held out for the more desirable silvers. Once our limits were taken care of, we got comfortable in the boat and began "helping" Easten as we ate sandwiches and drank soda pop.

Easten had caught more fish than any of us, but he had yet to connect on a silver. He couldn't get his line back in after a cast without a chum or pink on his hook—mostly pinks. After an hour or so of landing pinks his cast and retrieve would be punctuated with "Oh no, not another pink."

It wasn't long until Andy started helping us help Easten. Each time Easten hooked a pink, Andy would sing "Hi-Ho Humpie," and we'd all laugh. All except Easten. He was getting frustrated, but took the friendly ribbing in stride.

Finally, Andy suggested we move to another hole and see if Easten's luck would change. It didn't. And Andy continued his "Hi-Ho Humpie" serenade. It wasn't long before Easten's good-natured smile disappeared and he started fishing in concentrated earnest.

Easten was about ready to call it a day when a silver finally hit his lure, but his good fortune was short-lived as the silver was soon celebrating its freedom by jumping and shaking Easten's spinner at him—of course, less any attached line.

A few casts later, sandwiched between Andy's "Hi-Ho Humpie" concerts, Easten finally regained a portion of his ego with the landing of a silver. With the netting of his first silver, his courage came back and he decided to continue fishing. His bad luck returned with his courage and Andy's "Hi-Ho Humpie" song became more frequent until time run out and mercifully saved Easten from further embarrassment.

Of course the ribbing didn't end with Easten putting away his rod. It continued until Andy said goodbye and called one more "Hi-Ho Humpie" to Easten as we departed the river. Even after we got home and reported our trip to the family, we smiled and sang "Hi-Ho Humpie."

I'm surprised, however, that Easten hasn't remembered his and my last silver fishing trip with Andy Couch. It was a couple of years ago. Easten and Andy caught all the fish and I was the one who didn't fit in. I didn't even catch a pink so Andy could sing, "Hi-Ho Humpie."

Homestead to
Alaska and Back

Near a small side creek, in a deep channel next to the bank, the river slows in a triangular shape. John, the guide, maneuvers the boat to put the lures next to the edge of the gravel bar. It begins to rain.

"Fish like to stay on the back end of that gravel bar. We will ease to the left and put our lures out with a long line so we can cover a lot of ground."

John instructs his client, Jim Sanders, from Homestead Florida, to let the line out nine turns of the level wind mechanism to bring the lures about 50 feet behind the boat. He then starts trolling back and forth across the area where he thinks fish live. When a fish strikes, he maneuvers the boat sideways so the angler can fight the fish without tangling up.

John knows where the channels are. In low water he must be very careful. The waters of the Kvichak are big and he knows his client must be patient. Late-fall rainbow fishing is not like salmon fishing.

"Fish on!" Jim shouts as the hook is set. One hundred feet behind the boat a huge rainbow breaks water as the rain lets up. Jim cannot gain line, since the fish is large and strong enough to hold its own. Making two hard runs the fish strips out line, increases the distance between itself and the boat, and enters even faster water.

The large river-wise rainbow is no match for Jim's angling ability. The rain suddenly ceases. Off to the west the sun begins to break through the rain clouds as the distance between fish and angler closes. As Jim brings his catch within netting or releasing distance, the sun and rain clouds combine in a phenomenal rainbow over the river.

"Do you want to net this fish?" John asks, meaning, did Jim want to keep it. John nets only the fish his clients intend to keep for trophies because he does not want to injure the fish. To facilitate a clean release when a fish is not kept, he leans over and takes the hook out of its mouth while it is still in the water.

"This is the one. Yes, we're going to keep it. It's my trophy. I knew this was my fish because of the way he fought and he's also the biggest fish I've caught on this trip. A beautiful fish, I think he will make a good mount with a lot of good memories," Jim explains.

"This is a once-in-a-lifetime situation and I thank God for the opportunity I've had this week. I don't know if that full-circle rainbow to the west was a signal from heaven approving of my actions, but it worked out real nice. How much prettier could you have it in a place like this, and then catch a beautiful fish like that, and the rainbow; it was unbelievable."

Jim continues in the mood created by the capture of his trophy and what seemed like an omen from heaven with the timely creation of the western rainbow. "There is more here than fishing. Alaska really does something for me. It is wild and uncivilized and the rivers are clean. This just can't be beat."

Then, realizing the serious turn the conversation has taken and feeling a bit embarrassed by having expressed his personal thoughts, Jim lightens up with, "I just get the guide trained and I have to go home to Homestead."

Hovercraft Kings

It was early morning when 8-year-old Easten and I met our hovercraft pilot, or captain, at the mouth of Ship Creek. I never know whether we're flying or boating so I don't know whether the man in charge is a captain or a pilot. Our invitation was to fish Theodore Creek on the west side of Cook Inlet using a new hovercraft as transportation. We must have been a little tardy as they were ready to go immediately upon our arrival.

Having never been on a hovercraft, neither Easten nor I knew what to expect and we were surprised when the engine began turning. The craft made more noise than we expected and dirty, muddy water sprayed out and up from the bottom fans. The pilot eased the machine into the flat water of the inlet and soon we were sailing or flying, whatever it is you do when the hovercraft begins to move. It was quite exciting in spite of the noise and spray.

"There's the mouth of the Little Susitna River," the pilot exclaimed above the noise, and pointed to a low spot in the inlet's bank. "We're just coming up on the Big Su now." As the pilot announced that we were coming up on the Big Susitna River the engine in the hovercraft made a mighty roar and at the same time the machine settled on the water and our forward speed quickly went to a crawl.

The pilot shut down all engines and sought to find out the problem. "The shaft that drives the lower fan is broke," he said. "We're not going very far now."

The captain made some mechanical adjustments and restarted the engine. We could plow forward, but were unable to get on the step. We were now a boat, a slow-moving boat.

A small, slow-moving boat in the middle of Cook Inlet with the second highest tide in North America flowing at an increasingly higher speed. Fortunately, the tide was coming in and pushed us toward the Little Su.

Without too much trouble the captain guided our disabled craft out of the inlet and up the river. As the tide increased in intensity our captain guided the hovercraft upriver until we came to Susitna Station. Susitna Station was abandoned except for Wendell the caretaker, who met us at the boat dock and invited us to come in for lunch. During lunch it was decided that Easten and I would go fishing and our captain would use Wendell's phone and arrange for a mechanic and transportation back to Anchorage.

It was a warm summer day. Fishing for kings on the Little Su didn't hold much promise but Easten and I went through the motions. We were fishing with Wendell's salmon egg concoction, but I just knew it wouldn't have made any difference if we'd used a bare hook or no hook at all. We'd have had the same results.

I plunked my bait into the hole's middle and propped the rod between cracks in the dock. After a few minutes I wandered off the dock and Wendell and I began swapping fish tales. Wendell was halfway through an exciting story when Easten walked up. I could tell he had something on his mind, but he was courteous and held back until Wendell finished. Finally Wendell ran down and Easten spoke up.

"Dad, I think you've got a fish on your line!"

I looked and sure enough, there was my rod tip bouncing like a Michael Jordan dribble. By the time I reached the dock's end the butt of my rod had nearly worked its way out of the crack, but I was just in time. It was a long battle, but with Easten's encouragement, I landed a nice-size, ocean-fresh Little Susitna king.

Of course we didn't get to the Theodore, and never have. It was the last time we sailed or flew a hovercraft. However, it wasn't the last time for Little Susitna fishing for Easten and me, but the hovercraft King was the most unique.

Iliamna Fishing Competition

Mark Eaton fishes the "off season." The "off season" for the 7-foot-4-inch center for the Utah Jazz is the on season for fishing. He has a mentor in the form of neighbor John Beck. John is in the fishing tackle business. He's in the business as an excuse to fish. John is a fishaholic. Mark says John is an addict. "He's a great friend as well as fishing partner. He has taught me many things, including what a rod should feel like, and how to read the water on a stream, or in a lake. John has got me to the point where I can consistently catch nice size browns and rainbows." Many a quiet off-season early morning (20 to 30 times a year) will find coach John and pupil Mark casting in the streams near their home at the foot of Utah's Park City ski runs.

Two weeks before basketball training began, Mark and John did a little workout of their own in Alaska. Mark came for fall rainbows. Wisely, he brought his coach with him.

John proved two things to the guides, pilots, and other lodge guests. One: the right gear, used properly by skilled hands, by an experienced and serious fisherman, will catch more and bigger fish. Two: properly trained by a qualified coach, given a little luck, the student will outfish the instructor.

For most of the week it appeared the coach would win the league. Fish were caught by both fishermen each day and in every water fished. But John did catch the first one every day, the most, and the biggest. Mark stayed in the game, but it looked like John would take the pennant.

John's lead came on the second day by landing a 15-pound rainbow on the Kvichak river. What a battle it was. What fun, to hook a steelhead-size native rainbow, overcome him with skill and strategy, and release him to thrill another angler, another day.

John Beck's face disappeared behind a smile that was all teeth as he held and hugged his trophy rainbow. The release became a halftime event. In almost total silence they watched as the fish regained the strength expended in battle and his composure lost at losing. With cheerleader-like shouts, the anglers watched the big 'bow disappear under the floats of the airplane and back to the main channel.

The grand finale came in the final minutes of play. It happened on the Newhalen River, next to the Iliamna airport. With only minutes left on the clock before boarding the plane, Mark hooked into what became the fish that won the season title for him. He took more than 30 minutes to land this late-in-the-game rainbow. It was taken on 4-pound test line, weighed 16 pounds, and was 33 inches long.

With the catch and release of this magnificent once-in-a-life-time trophy, Mark won the playoffs. But John, you're still coach of the year, and there is always next season.

Buy Him Tad Pollys

by Margaret Swensen

My man is a fisherman. I mean FISHERMAN in capital letters. I listen to stories about strikes, lagoons, cut banks, backwater, and feeding frenzies. I don't understand all I hear, but the guy seems to know what he's talking about and the light in his eyes is dime bright.

My man is a man for all seasons. The season of char, pike, Dollies, rainbow, grayling, and all species of salmon. His fingers have been cut, frozen, bruised, line-burned, and stuck with hooks. When I ask about his injuries, he always says, "It's nothin' honey." His feet are constantly wet during fishing season, his hair needs cutting and his beard grows unheeded.

I don't buy him new clothes for the special days of his life, Christmas or birthdays. I buy him Pixies, Maribou, Tad Pollys, and Spin-N-Glos. The shirt I bought him, the latest in fashion, just hangs in the closet; but the plaid wool Pendleton I have mended again and again, is his everyday favorite.

Posturepedic by Sealy means nothing to him. If it isn't polypropylene and nestling in spruce boughs or on a sandy beach, it isn't comfort. His idea of gourmet cooking is fresh catch sprinkled with ashes and basted in morning bacon excess.

He talks about Kasilof, Tikchik, Iliamna, and Ninilchik. The bumper sticker, "Where the hell is Chitna?" makes him want to go fishing again.

Once when he spoke so excitedly of the big one, I thought he was taking me to the big one at the mall—you know the sale of the year. How silly of me. No-o, he was talking kings — not rings and things!

I'm getting acquainted with names of those things he ties on the end of fishing string. I thought "Alaska Mary Ann" and

"Oakie Drifter" were fishing buddies. One day, he dragged them out of his tackle box and tried to explain what they were. I looked, but all I could see was a bag of eggs from some mother fish who was probably worried about her little ones.

The other day I was quietly reading my Good Housekeeping magazine and he hollers from the garage, "Honey, do you know where I left my Butt Skunk?" The page blurred before my eyes. Was I supposed to slap him or ask what naughty magazine he was reading?

I miss him when he's gone fishing. I wonder if the weather will let him come home according to plan. I know he would be overjoyed to get two or three more days of fishing because of moody Mother Nature. His boss, a real fisherman himself, won't mess with Mother Nature either, so I know my man won't lose his job.

Change him? Never. Some day he will say, "I love you more than going fishing." I couldn't ask for more.

Newspaper Salmon

I received a call one day from the president of a large corporation located in the South-48. Seems they wanted to hold a board of directors meeting in a fishing lodge in Alaska during the height of the red run. The president wanted me to recommend a place where they could go that could accommodate 20 people. After I gave a few suggestions, the president let me know that he was getting ready for the following year. What he wanted to do was bring two men with him this year and check out the places I suggested and make sure they would work for their group.

He asked me to charter a plane and meet him on a given day and we'd fly all over Southwest Alaska looking at luxury lodges for the right one for his board of directors. And so it was that the president, his meeting coordinator, the company security chief, and I found ourselves on a Ketchum floatplane flying through Lake Clark Pass on a clear day with Craig Ketchum as pilot.

Our first stop was Van Valin's lodge located on an island on Lake Clark. The lodge, surrounded by water, immediately won the approval of Security, but received low marks by Coordinator because of the meeting-room size. President never said one way or the other.

Next we flew to Kirk Gay's Valhalla Lodge on SIx Mile Lake. Coordinator liked the lodge's individual cabins and large meeting area, but Security didn't like the possibility that folks from Nondalton could drop in and maybe spoil the meeting—especially since many of the village's residents were hunters and would be carrying loaded guns when the meeting was held. President again remained noncommittal.

From Valhalla, we flew to Sara Hornberger's Koksetna Camp where we ate lunch. Koksetna Camp, with its windmill-powered electric system and all natural bathroom facilities, won high marks by both Security and Coordinator: President didn't say how he liked it, but everyone agreed that Sara Hornberger's newspaper salmon lunch was about the best fish they'd ever tried, and that kind of cooking gained the lodge at least ten points toward being selected as the board of directors meeting site.

The last lodge on our visiting list was Iliamna Lake Resort. Iliamna Lake Resort, a large complex of duplex-style log cabins surrounding a common area lawn, is on a road between two villages. Before Security could complain about hunters with guns coming from both directions, and Coordinator pointing out the difficulty of getting from the rooms to the meeting area, President said he liked it, and they'd hold their meeting there. That ended the discussion that never started. President liked it and all of a sudden Security and Coordinator liked it.

As it turned out, however, they decided to hold the board of directors meeting at the company's home office. There was a downturn in business and President didn't want to offend his stockholders and employees by meeting at a fishing lodge when the company was laying people off and not paying a dividend. "Not smart PR," he said.

It was interesting to me to see how the captains of industry pick their meeting sites, but it did make me wonder, since President made his decision without consulting with Coordinator or Security, why he brought them along. I also wonder what the stockholders would think about spending their dividend for President, Security, Coordinator, and me to fly around Alaska all day with Craig Ketchum visiting $500-a-day fishing lodges.

It was worth the day for me to go along. I saw lots of good country, met nice folks, and obtained the recipe for Sara Hornberger's newspaper salmon and the best use of the Anchorage Daily News. Just take a cleaned salmon, remove the head and tail and wrap it in ten layers of wet newspaper and bake it in the oven, on a cookie sheet or large cake pan, for one hour at 350 degrees. It'll be some of the best salmon you'll ever eat, and it'll put the Anchorage Daily News to good use.

The Real Shore Lunch

Not all fishing trips to luxury lodges end up being luxury fishing trips. I was fishing out of Kokhanok Falls Lodge, which had just changed ownership. The new owner invited me to "come on out for a fishing trip of a lifetime." And so the date and time were scheduled and I soon found myself getting off an Era airplane in Iliamna, and along with 50 other anglers, searching for our guides.

The most experienced-looking guide, from the group of guides looking for their clients, stepped up and asked, "Are you Evan? Get your gear and we'll drive to the plane and go to the lodge."

I'd been to Kokhanok Falls Lodge before. Before it opened that spring the new owner hired me and my filming crew to make a promotion video for the lodge. We had enough stock footage for the action parts of the video, but nothing of the lodge itself. We chartered Ketchum Air Service to fly us to the lodge, where we spent the day filming for the promotion video. It was too early for fishing so the trip was strictly a working trip.

My return to Kokhanok was still a little early for salmon, but Dolly and rainbow fishing were supposed to be excellent, and they would be the target species. I was accompanied by Alaska first-timers Mark Eaton, of the Utah Jazz, and his neighbor, John Beck.

When we arrived at the lodge we noticed we were the only guests. Our pilot-guide and the cook were the only employees at the lodge. We suspected other guests would arrive later.

The first few days were what you'd expect from a $500-a-day luxury fishing lodge. We flew to a new location each day, sometimes more than one location. We tried Talarik Creek and Kvichak River plus a couple of Dream Creeks and No-tell-um Creeks—secret spots known only to our guide. All in all—except there were no other guests to share fishing tales with in the evening—the trip was a great trip up until the last day. Actually it stayed a great trip, but it turned different from any trip I've had before, or for that matter, since.

As we climbed aboard our deHavilland Beaver the final morning, the guide told us that we'd be going to a new spot for Dollies and the cook would be joining us. And with a smile he said, "And you've got to catch your own lunch." as we placed our rods behind the seats.

Not long after our arrival at the fishing hole we caught parts of a conversation between the cook and guide and discovered that the guide meant what he'd said. The lodge was out of food. For some reason the food plane had not arrived as scheduled and if we wanted to eat, we had to catch our own lunch.

Fortunately the guide put us in the right spot, the fish were friendly, and the cook knew how to fix a shore lunch. I've had many shore lunches before; some were prepared with great fanfare and even included fine China and linen tablecloths. And, I've caught my own lunch before—many times. But this was the first time I was forced to fish to eat, and it sure put a new meaning to subsistence and a new slant on fishing from a luxury lodge. And, I'll be the first to confess, it was the best shore lunch I've ever eaten.

Closed, Gone Fishing

I recall as a boy seeing a movie about a small-town doctor who did a lot of good for the local young people. Most of it was accomplished out on the riverbank drowning worms during office hours. The community leaders, led by the banker with whom a loan was past due, were always after him to shape up and tend to his practice. When the collector came calling, the doctor was away with several boys on the riverbank and there was a sign on his office door, *Closed. Gone fishing.*

Rumor has it that when the sun shines in Southeast Alaska everyone closes up and goes fishing. Petersburg claims 37 rain-free days per year and outdoorsmen from drier climates would excuse the truancy and probably even encourage it.

I suspect the dream of every fisherman is to put a sign on the door occasionally and let the world know that for at least one day a year priorities are right. For several years the folks at Alaska Sausage Company would close down for a day and put a *Closed, Gone Fishing* sign on the door. The staff, management, spouses, and friends packed it up and headed for water.

I was privileged to join Alaska Sausage Owner, Herb Eckman, and his employees one year for a *Closed, Gone Fishing* outing on rivers and streams along Big Susitna River. It was a great day of contests, prizes, and fishing fun. I was saddened when I learned that they don't have their *Closed, Gone Fishing* day anymore.

I was fishing out of Rainbow Bay Resort with a couple of anglers from Outside. They were mostly fishing and I was mostly taking pictures. I had captured their fishing successes on several rolls of 35 mm film and envisioned putting their pictures and story in Alaska Outdoors magazine. One of the men gladly signed my model release, but when I asked his partner for a release to put his picture in Alaska Outdoors magazine, he said, "No way. Don't even think about putting my picture anyplace." He then got together with his fishing buddy and in just a few minutes his buddy asked for his model release back and asked me not to publish their story or put any pictures in the magazine.

Later I learned that they had been assigned by their company to work in Anchorage, and their time spent out fishing was probably not authorized by their employer. They just got to thinking about being in Alaska and couldn't stand not wetting a line and decided to be Closed, Gone Fishing.

There have been a great number of Closed Gone Fishing Days during my four decades in Alaska, and I suspect you've had a few days when you called in sick and went fishing. I'll tell you what—let's start planning right now and you and I set a date to put a sign on our office door next summer and let everyone know, that for at least one day we've got our priorities right, and that we're *Closed, Gone Fishing*.

Fly Rod Diplomacy

For years guns of the Soviet Union, only three miles from Little Diomede Island, Alaska, were aimed at the United States. Siberia-based Russian missiles, 37 miles from St. Lawrence Island, Alaska, pointed their payload westward toward America. United States Air Force pilots regularly intercepted Soviet aircraft flying in American airspace. Guns, planes, and missiles patrolled and protected the two countries' only common border. Communication between governments was so strained that talk stopped and deadly defense took over, leaving two superpowers to bark and threaten each other across a pencil line drawn on a piece of paper.

While the heads of state were shaking their fists at each other, Trout Unlimited and its counterpart in Russia got together to share their pastime of fishing. They hoped their exchange would result in a breaking down of borders and prejudices, and open up common communication. Communication where heads of state meet and discuss world matters while fishing. Prejudices reduced to differences of opinion on which fly to use to trick a trout. They wanted to see border battles fought as a friendly fishing contest, both sides the winner.

They were somewhat successful with their fly rod diplomacy as East met West with the common denominator of fishing, barriers, boundaries, and borders broke down. Communication and understanding replaced mistrust and differences disappeared—and the Berlin wall fell.

Trout Unlimited's fly rod diplomacy reminded me that what may work on a national and international scale will work at home. If you've got a youngster you can't communicate with,

213

take him fishing. Take them one on one. Let them talk. You listen. Don't judge or condemn. Just listen. You'll be saying more to your child by listening than all the talking, all the shouting, or all the threats you can make or have made. Every week can be Take-a-Kid-Fishing Week and it really isn't necessary to catch fish to have fun. What is important is that every chance you get, take your kid fishing.

If child could meet parent with the common denominator of fishing, barriers, boundaries, and borders would break down. Communication and understanding would replace mistrust and differences would disappear.

I'll bet you get satisfying results. I think it will even work with wives, mothers-in-law, fellow employees, and neighbors.

Spring Diggings

I had never really thought about it, but one day I got to wondering if a clam was happy at high tide or low tide. I've heard people say they were as happy as a clam at one of the tides, I just couldn't remember which tide.

What prompted this cogitation in the first place was a call from my friend, Dave Hilderbrand. Dave said, "Come for dinner and don't be late. The wife's got clams and they are good only if they're hot."

Instantly I recalled a bygone day when someone who represented himself as being on my side, dropped a gunnysack full of clams on the front step late one evening. I spent the entire night cleaning the fool things.

Opening the shells and taking the insides out, I made two piles. One pile of what I thought was the good stuff, one pile of everything else. By the time I got them cleaned and the piles separated, I couldn't eat either one. I ended up giving the clams to a neighbor who just loved them. I guess he got the right pile.

At the Hilderbrands', Dave said, "Sit right down. Here's a large napkin. You will need it. Help yourself to the salad. I'll bring in the clams."

When I saw the platter of clams on the table I decided I must be the subject of a joke. The clams still had their shells on. I was told to pry them open, pull out the meat with the fork, dip it in butter, and just let him slide down.

I thought to myself, "Not on your life, Hilderbrand! I am not putting that in my mouth." As I stared with shock, the whole family opened up shells, pulled out the meat, dipped it in butter, and almost with ritual, slid it across the taste buds and down the hatch.

Well, I'd read Robert Service's *Ice Worm Cocktail* and they were not making a fool out of me. I played the joke to the end. I proceeded with the same pomp and ceremony as my host. As my mouth opened, my eyes automatically closed. "Stomach, please stay down."

I knew they were all waiting for the joke to spring. I just let the thing slip across my lips. What a surprise. It was really good. No! Better than that. Delicious!

I opened my eyes. No one was watching me or even caring. The platter was drying up and the shell plate was filling up.

After dinner I asked Dave, "Where did all those clams come from?"

Dave explained how he and his son spent the last Saturday digging butter clams. I now know about butter clams. They are different from the razor clams deposited on my step ages ago.

On my first butter-clam-digging outing, it came to me sitting on the beach in one of the coves in Kachemak Bay. The clam has got to be happy when the digger is not. Happy digger. Unhappy clams.

This spring you can write it down and underscore it. I'll be on the beach digging. Happy as a clam at high tide. The neighbors will have to dig their own. I'm keeping mine.

Turnagain Tide Tragedy

Prior to the Great Alaska Earthquake, when Alaska was for Alaskans, the land along the shore of Turnagain Arm was as much as eight feet higher than it is now. The earthquake slipped the earth's crust, allowing the land at the mouth of Twentymile River to sink. Before the earthquake I fished the area many times a season. A one-hour drive from Anchorage would put me on the creek. Ten minutes to slip the boat from its trailer and load up our gear, and another 15 minutes of river travel put us at an excellent silver-fishing hole at the junction of Twentymile and its first clear-water tributary.

Max Marquiss and I arrived at the fishing hole in the early evening. As we pulled into the tributary and slid the boat up on the beach we discovered the water was boiling with migrating silver salmon. It was an evening when we almost had to bait our hook from behind a tree to keep the fish off until we could cast. In our exuberance we forgot the time and fished until it was dark.

Wanting to stay over and catch the morning's first fishing we justified staying by making the excuse that we didn't want to go on the river at night. We pulled the 12-foot boat up on the beach, propped it on its side for a lean-to, built a fire in front, and cooked a fresh-caught silver for dinner. Using spruce boughs for a bed we slept until it was light.

With the first light of morning we noticed that the water in the stream had come up during the night. We paid it little attention and went about fishing. Finally running out of time, we left the stream so we could return home in time for work.

When we arrived back at our car we discovered that it had

been flooded by the tide. We learned that the year's highest tide had occurred that night. Fortunately, water did not get into the gas tank, but the engine and seats had been covered. Portage, a little town in those days, had a couple of service stations where we were able to get kerosene and oil. We drained the crankcase and flushed it out with kerosene, then filled it with oil. The engine started up and we let it run for a few minutes. We then reflushed it with kerosene and refilled the crankcase with oil, and sitting on wet seats we returned to Anchorage.

Immediately on our return, the car was taken to a service station and given the full treatment. It was run through the car wash several times. It seemed to run all right, and except for a foul interior smell, it appeared that we had escaped with only a minor expense and a little inconvenience. With the coming of winter we soon learned we were mistaken. At the first day of freezing weather we found that water had gotten into many places and it remained even after service. Things that were supposed to slide didn't. Windows wouldn't roll up or down. The transmission wouldn't shift, the interior fogged up and then froze, restricting our vision.

Toward summer, when it seemed that all was well and we were now past any crisis, inconvenience turned to tragedy. First, the U-joints broke, then door window handles refused to work, and finally the front wheels fell off. Upon careful examination we discovered that almost everything covered by the salt water of Turnagain Arm was rusted away or corroded beyond use or repair. We had to junk the car.

I've only been back up Twentymile once since the earthquake. The gravel beaches we fished from and camped on are now covered with mud. Because the land has lowered, the beach is now tide affected. No longer can Max and I siwash it on Twentymile and fish all night for silvers, even if we remembered to keep our car above the tide line.

Shell's Silvers

Once, while fishing the mouth of the Talachulitna River, the fishing stopped dead cold. Steve Johnson, my guide, suggested we move across Skwentna River and try the mouth of Shell Creek.

Shell Creek is a small stream draining Shell Lake. It enters the Skwentna River 300 yards downriver from the mouth of the Tal and on the other side of the river. A sandbar in the Skwentna at the mouth of Shell Creek grows and recedes with the season. Sometimes it nearly blocks the passage of Shell Creek. When this happens a small lake develops behind the sandbar and at times this lake becomes a shallow water holding area for traveling silvers.

Steve led me to the sandbar and the mouth of Shell Creek. Another party was already fishing the hole. Steve moved me around a stand of trees, now in three feet of water because of the sandbar growth. He pointed to a patch of water I would never have fished had I not been directed to do so. For an hour I caught and released silvers, one after another. Meanwhile, the other group left the good, but now unproductive hole.

When our upper spot behind the trees cooled down the lower hole was ready for another try. Thirty or more silvers cruised around and across the 40-foot diameter pool. I again followed Steve's instruction and connected time and time again. The afternoon proved to be one of my most productive silver days.

From my home I can see Mt. Susitna and the Alaska Range beyond. Somewhere between Susitna and the perennially snow-covered peaks of the Alaska Range flows a little stream out of Shell Lake. Although I can't see it from my home, I know it's there, and when fall comes I long to warm up the mouth of Shell Creek.

Alaska Outdoor's Other Side

Outdoor's Other Side

Time was when I think I had myself convinced my fishing and hunting excursions were to provide meat for the winter. The bounty of Alaska's outdoors has filled cans, bottles, and freezer since my first cast in the Russian River. The legal limit was six salmon per day with a two-day possession limit. About every other day we would drive to the Russian after work and walk the two miles to our favorite hole. Having great confidence in our ability to fish and the river's capacity to provide, we would build a fire. Once the fire was set, we would break out our rods.

Fish were stacked on top of each other and it didn't take long to bring the first salmon in. Whoever was fortunate enough to draw first catch would immediately clean the fish, wrap it in foil, and put it under the coals of the fire. We'd then fish for a couple of hours, and fill our limit

By then the fire would be just a warm spot on the ground in the center of a circle of rocks. The foil wrapped around our first-caught salmon was now blackened by the coals. Someone would fish it out with a stick and unwrap the package. The perfectly cooked sockeye would be laid out on a log. We'd then help ourselves to gourmet "Red à la riverbank."

Next, we'd throw sleeping bags under one of the giant spruce trees crowding the shore and take a few minutes of sleep. With the coming of dawn the cast-hook-play-land-clean-and put-in-the-pack process began again. As soon as the new day's limit was stored, each would shoulder packs and hike to the car for the drive home. A day later we would repeat the process and continue until we considered we had enough, or the run ran out.

Hunting season came almost concurrent with the decline of

the red run. Telling myself it was my duty to provide for my family, I would venture forth into the field in search of game. Every season closed with a moose or caribou or both tucked away as steaks, roasts, or sausage to grace our dinner table or snack tray until next spring and we began again the process of replenishing our larder.

We would hunt off the road around Skilak Lake, drive the highway to Lake Louise, or fly out and be dropped off along a riverbank sandbar. We seldom returned home empty-handed and thereby justified our excursion and left the door open for future time in Alaska's outdoors.

One year, after a successful Dall sheep hunt, I made the mistake of adding up the cost and figuring the amount per pound. Now that I know it costs $82.37 per pound to put sheep in the freezer, I'm having a difficult time convincing myself that I go hunting because "we need the meat."

Even at today's inflated supermarket prices I suspect if I put the pencil to it I would discover Russian River reds are more costly per pound than commercially caught fish sold at Carrs supermarket just down the street from my house.

Knowing this has not decreased the number of times I go hunting or fishing. It has just made me be honest with myself about the real reasons I go into the Alaska outdoors. I go fishing and never unpack my rod and many hunting trips end without firing a shot or even any honest hunting taking place. I admit to myself I go outdoors for the outdoors, that bagging game or landing a trophy is part of the experience, but only part of the experience, not the experience.

An early-morning walk on a deserted Kachemak Bay beach hunting colored rocks with my son, and bringing home a trophy to show mother is a real part of the Alaska outdoors. Digging clams and pulling crab and shrimp pots is part. Taking pictures, keeping a campfire going, or watching a beaver tackle a 24-inch-diameter cottonwood is part. Sometimes the most exciting thing to do is to do nothing. Taking time to just sit, relax, and enjoy the surroundings, breathe air so pure you can't see it, listen to the deafening silence of a still night, or feel the immense size of wilderness on a clear day with unlimited visibility is part of the whole that makes the real Alaska outdoor experience.

The real reason to go afield is found in the varied activities associated with the one we used as the contrived excuse to go. Long after the thrill of bagging a trophy is gone the other things remain and are rehearsed in our minds and storied to others.

I am not speaking for myself. I go outdoors in Alaska because it's my job. When others are enjoying their time afield and having fun—I'm working.

Alaska for Alaskans

My first summer outing in Alaska with my family was a drive-to-and-camp trip to McKinley Park in 1958. Notice I said McKinley Park. In those days, before the area was nationalized and called Denali, the park could be enjoyed by Alaskans.

We drove the Denali Highway from Paxson to Cantwell and then on into the park. It was fall and the countryside was alive with color and wildlife. Once in the park, we camped the first night under a huge spruce tree. Our meager budget did not allow us the luxury of tent or sleeping bags. We fashioned a lean-to shelter from a tarpaulin and spread our camping blankets over a spruce bough mattress. It rained during the night, but we enjoyed the sound of rain dripping from the spruce needles onto our tarp ceiling.

Before setting up camp, we checked with the park ranger. Different from the treatment we'd probably receive if we tried to repeat our trip today, the ranger was helpful, told us where we could camp, recommended we get up early and drive the park road to Wonder Lake, and pointed out on the map the spots were we were likely to see sheep, bear, moose, and caribou.

Somewhere in the last four decades it seems that the National Park Service has forgotten what a public servant is, who serves whom when a public servant comes in contact with the public, and even what the word service means in the name of their organization. It's too bad, too.

Our friendly 1958 ranger guided us through McKinley for a trip never to be forgotten nor repeated. Sheep were where the knowledgeable ranger said they would be. Bear and moose as well. Caribou roamed the side of the road in huge herds.

At one point we stopped the car and my 3-year-old son and I tried a caribou-stalking procedure tip told to us by the ranger. He said caribou were curious animals and if a white flag was waved in their direction, they would likely stop their grazing migration and "come on over and take a look."

We tied a white handkerchief to a stick and walked along with and toward the caribou herd. One of the animals on the outside of the moving river of caribou saw us. His head came up from his lichen grazing and he took a couple of steps toward us. Then the herd stopped. All at once we were the center of attention of at least two thousand eyes. The caribou would take a few steps in our direction, stop, sniff the wind, and then advance a few more feet.

We stopped, and held our white flag high. Having that many wild animal eyes staring us down was intimidating to us in our Alaska inexperience. For a moment it was exciting, then intimidating, and finally, downright scary as the herd moved closer and closer. We didn't know what to do, nor what they would do. We just stood our ground and held our white flag over our heads.

At some predestined distance, all the animals in concert stopped, raised their heads, reached their necks toward us for a better see and smell, and slowly, without fear, drifted back to grazing tundra. We watched a moment as they departed, and as our heartbeats returned to normal, we marched back to our car. By the time we reached the car the caribou had moved beyond our sight and we were left looking at empty country with no evidence that anything alive had ever been there, let alone over four thousand hooved feet marching to the wilderness dinner bell.

On my last visit to McKinley, we discovered that two things were noticeably different: the friendly ranger had been replaced by a new-generation keep-people-out-of-the-park ranger, and we didn't see but a few scattered caribou. You bet I hunger for the good old days when Alaska was for Alaskans.

Denali for Alaskans

Back in '58, when Alaska was a territory, and way before the Parks Highway spanned Hurricane Gulch, slashed its way through Broad Pass, and bridged the Susitna River, Alaskans drove the Denali Highway from Paxson to Cantwell and then on to McKinley National Park. We, like many new transplants to the Territory of Alaska, desired to see all of her wonders, the park being one of them. It was a time when Denali was also for Alaskans. A time before tourism took over.

During the first spring after Alaska became a state, we started planning a fall road trip to McKinley. On clear days we could see from Anchorage the perpetually snow-capped peak of McKinley off in the distance and craved to drive and camp as close as possible to the highest mountain on this continent. The first week in September found us with our three small children winding our way over the Denali Highway in our old Plymouth. Although it is four decades ago, it was an adventure never to be forgotten.

Details of the trip are vague, but what is clear is the beauty and grandeur of McKinley National Park. With tourism came buses, rules, restrictions, and even the name of McKinley changed to Denali. For some reason, Alaskans do not want to see Denali from a tour bus window and shown to them by a recent high school graduate from Outside. They want to travel Denali in the family car or motor home.

Each year the National Park Service gives Denali back to Alaskans for three days the week following the departure of the last organized tour in September. They allow a given number of private vehicles to drive the Denali Park Road and award the privilege by lottery. Lottery winners are allowed to drive the park road and soak up Denali at a pace they themselves set, and see the sights of most interest to them. They are not confined to a tour bus schedule or a young guide's passion. The National Park Service even backs off many of the rules and restrictions obviously designed to control a great number of summer visitors. And they put on their best "Welcome to Denali" smile and demeanor. It's wonderful.

My wife and I were lucky and drew a drive-Denali permit this September and visited the park together for the first time in four decades. Once past the short paved road to Savage River it seemed to us like we were back on the road of '58. Not much had changed. We were reminded of our Denali trek of '58, when we again witnessed the awesome beauty of Polychrome Pass, the abundance of wildlife, and of course, the majesty of McKinley, clothed in a wispy Victoria Secret-like cloud-nightgown. We were awed again to be looking up nearly five miles from Wonder Lake to the top of McKinley—the only place in America where a person can look up for five miles and see something still attached to Mother Earth.

We were allowed to begin our drive at 6 a.m. with the understanding that we must be back by midnight. At first we rebelled at the restriction, but once on the road it was obvious that a solid 18-hour absorbing of Denali in ideal fall weather and color was about all we could take in one sitting. By the time we returned to Park Headquarters we were maxed out. We could contain no more. We had to admit, "It is enough."

We spent two hours witnessing a grandfather-sized moose protect his harem of cows from six suitors who wanted to add their children to Denali's moose gene pool. But fear of the patriarch overcame their natural desires and they stayed their distance. While we watched, the young bulls practiced their fighting techniques on each other—the techniques they hone to perfection. One day one of them will become king of the harem, and the old bull will be put out to pasture. Other moose were spotted on sidehills and in distant meadows. A couple of caribou showed themselves and wandered away.

Dall sheep, too, came to the road to view. They wandered across the river valley from a high distant peak to display their beauty beside Denali Park Road for all to see and photograph.

Ptarmigan, squirrels, and other birds and mammals lost their shyness and came to be awed at and photographed. Even the heavens got into the act and changed the weather every hour so as to give the Alaskans a summer's weather rendition during their 18-hour stay in Denali.

Then came the lords of Denali: silvertipped grizzlies, three at a time, harvesting blueberries, and anything that would add to their fat for winter. One bear came to the front of our motor home, looked us right in the eye. For a moment he looked cute and cuddly, but he obviously didn't want us left with a teddybear impression. He showed his teeth, moved his head in a menacing manner, and his whole carriage said, "Don't mess with me." And we didn't even think about it. Fifteen bears in all came three at a time and modeled for our cameras.

When evening came and shadows fell on the valleys, we watched night settle on Denali. Our day, our Alaska day for Alaskans, was over, and we were filled to overflowing. We know that progress demands that things cannot remain as they were, that inevitably the National Park Service must increase the number of visitors to Denali. Their mission dictates the maximum number of visitors and minimum quality of experience. But for three days, it's Denali maximum for Alaskans. Our thanks to the folks at Denali who let us wander back to '58, to the time when Denali also was for Alaskans.

Denali Then and Now

Back in '58, Margaret and I packed our old Plymouth with camping gear and our two babies and drove the Denali Highway to McKinley National Park. It was before the Parks Highway, and Denali was the only way in. There were few hunters on the road, just an occasional rubbernecking tourist like us.

For most of its 130-some-odd miles length, Denali Highway follows a low ridge providing travelers sweeping vistas of Alaska's wilderness finery. It's a gravel road. If it's wet, there's mud. If it's dry, there's dust. Whether it's dust or mud, it's washboard most of the way. You can't hurry on the Denali. If you do, your vehicle will pay the price for your unwise pushing the pedal.

But that was the beauty of traveling Denali. You had to go slowly to keep the dust down, the mud off your windshield, and your car's fenders from falling off. In the process you enjoyed the scenery and the wildlife. And you enjoyed it without a lot of traffic trying to gain four seconds on the car in front by risking their occupants' lives and yours by passing when it wasn't safe. Denali's character demanded you go slowly, see the sights, and enjoy your trip. Denali wasn't just a road to get from here to there—Denali was a destination in itself. A 130-mile-long destination, and as tall and wide as the horizon on both sides of the road and in the distance ahead.

Going as slowly as Denali demanded even gave travelers an opportunity to spot berry patches and wildlife from the front seat. Denali wasn't a drive-as-fast-as-you-can-to-get-there road you could master in three hours. It was a slow-down-and-enjoy road, taking at least all day, depending on how many berry patches were found or caribou or other critters spotted.

Our first trip in was on a sunny day, and dusty, and it took most of the day to consume the road—lots of berry patch stops and wildlife delays. We camped for the night in the park, and drove the road to Wonder Lake the next day, camping there and enjoying the land beneath McKinley. The third day of our trip found us back on the Denali Highway in rain—and mud, but enjoying Denali in reverse as much as we did going in.

Last summer, Margaret and I took Denali again for the first time in more than 40 years. Not much has changed on Denali. There's still mud and dust and washboards. But, more importantly, there's still berry patches, caribou, solitude, and country as wide and as far as you can see.

We noticed two changes to Denali, one: there were no motor homes or camp trailers on Denali in '58, and two: someone approached us with a minor emergency and asked a question which would never have been asked back then; "Have you got a telephone?"

We hope those are the only two changes that ever happen to Denali. One change we sure don't want to see is to blacktop it. There just has to be at least one place in Alaska where you can go and live the good old days. Denali's one place where you can, and I hope it never changes. I love Denali's mud, dust, berries, and beauty. When I go there again, even if it takes another 40 years to get there, I'd like it to be the same as it was back in '58.

CAVU

Outdoor adventures in the far north demand a different attitude than adventures elsewhere. Outdoorsmen must adapt their mental makeup to cope with 24-hour daylight and bugs. Insects can be more than just pesky, they can literally drive a person over the brink.

Once an outdoorsman is properly outfitted with a good quality bug-proof tent, head net, and lots of mosquito dope he can manage the bugs and they become just a mild annoyance. Often a breeze is blowing which keeps the bugs at bay.

Adventuring in the land of the midnight sun can be a challenging, but satisfying experience. Pitching a tent as the sun sets in the north at midnight, and watching it rise again in the north before last night's fire is cold, can be exciting. Sunsets blend into sunrises, and days are marked, not by darkness, but by twilight. An adventurer taking a late-afternoon nap on a warm hillside in the sun is often surprised when it cannot be determined if it is 10 a.m. or 10 p.m.

I once interviewed a young couple who went on an extended canoe trip around June 21, the longest day of the year. They were not in a hurry and decided to refrain from using a watch and just go as they desired without constraint of time. They slept when tired, moved when the mood struck them, and ate when hungry. Because of the expanded amount of daylight and twilight with no darkness, they lost all track of time and could not determine which day it was or if it was morning or afternoon. Getting back to civilization's time-controlled environment required some adjustment.

Then, of course, there's winter when darkness is supreme. Not real darkness however—darkness overcome by the lesser of God's heavenly bodies: moon, stars, and faraway planets, and punctuated by dazzling displays of the aurora borealis. Light reflected for millions of miles to arrive at an outdoor adventurer's camp to add beauty and wonder to a lonely campfire, or to add class to a heated can-of-beans lunch.

Outdoor adventures in Alaska are high adventure at the top of the world, where the air is clean and clear. A visitor, getting off the airline, looked around and said, "There must be something wrong with your air in Alaska—I can't see it."

Pilots receiving current weather reports before taking off, often hear the flight service attendant describe visibility as CAVU, clear and visibility unlimited. Someone from even a mildly smog-infested area cannot comprehend having unlimited visibility. Air so clear and unpolluted that mountain peaks 200 miles away appear to be an afternoon's jaunt away. Distances seem greater because of the isolation. Not only do outdoor adventurers go back to a time not governed by clocks, but they journey to a land where even the air allows freedom to look to the horizon and beyond.

Friends, Family, and a Fire

Very few things in life turn out as planned: Yesterday, last week, last month, or even last year. Fishing or hunting trips seldom go exactly as scheduled nor do they always end up with a full freezer. As an example, my daughter, Diane, and I were hunting goats just before her 18th birthday. It rained a steady downpour the entire second day of the hunt. A cold wind blew rain against us with such force our raingear finally surrendered and let the water in. We became so cold it hurt. Finally we could stand it no longer. At five in the afternoon we gave up and pitched our tent, deciding to just hole up and get dry and warm, thinking tomorrow had to be a better day.

No sooner was the tent up, than the rain doubled its intensity and wind picked up to gale force, driving the rain under the fly and right through the tent walls. We woke about midnight cold and wet. It made for a long, miserable night with very little sleep.

Another time I was hunting with my son, Alan. Our success in five days of hard hunting was a two-second view of the west end of an eastbound goat.

Several years ago I took two co-workers hunting. We flew out in my old Stinson on skis. After spending two days and a night we decided to move camp. Immediately after takeoff I ran out of altitude, airspeed, and ideas all at once. In the resulting crash we sustained injuries, but nothing life-threatening or permanent. The airplane was wrecked and my pride was seriously hurt.

These three failed hunting trips of yesterday really turned out to be successes now that it's tomorrow. Like the night in the wet tent with Diane. At first light we climbed out of the sack, wrung at least a gallon of icy water from each sleeping bag, and headed down the mountain to timber. Locating a perfect campsite, we made a leanto, built a fire, got warm, and slept for the balance of the day. For the next two days we dried out gear. Although no more rain came in our camp the mountain where the goats were was constantly fogged in.

We didn't fire a shot the entire week, but it was one of our most memorable hunting trips. Enduring the cold and wet let us discover things about ourselves and each other. We learned lessons about our abilities, our capabilities, and our frailties. I gained a greater respect for my teenage daughter. Her self-confidence increased. Some of the generation gap was closed.

The weather on the next to last day of the goat-hunting trip with Alan was terrible. We left camp anyway hoping this would be our day. In a steady downpour we headed for the top of the mountain, climbing between breaks in the fog.

Sometime after noon, as if by some orchestrated signal, the rain stopped and the fog broke. Sunlight burst across the valleys below and around us. We were surrounded by a rain-washed world. Bright sunlit contrasts of white and blue glaciers against the varied shades of green, combined with the variegated colors of nature to produce an indescribable, awe-inspiring setting.

The impact of the transformation of Mother Earth was so great and so sudden we could not even speak. We were in a giant auditorium and the stage was all around us. Everywhere we looked the scene erupted with beauty. We didn't even want to speak. Words would have desecrated the moment.

My hunting companions in the crashed Stinson proved to be real sportsmen and friends. They did not file lawsuits or make threats. They were sensitive to my lost airplane and injured pride. They did not place blame or cast judgement. The airplane was not salvageable, but through their kindness, my feelings were repaired.

Time healed the wounded pride and the airplane was replaced. My hunting partners made me a gift of a new rifle to replace the one broken in the crash. I use this gun each hunting season. It serves as a constant reminder, not of the wreck, but of two hunters who were also great sportsmen.

Sarkis Atamian's book, *The Bears of Manley*, is filled with stories of failed hunts, some even life-threatening failures, but in the end they turned out alright, as did my failed hunts. As I think back, those failed hunts are my most memorable. I've forgotten about the wet and cold, the busted and broken; all I remember now is the association with my son and daughter, companionship of two good friends, the Creator's majesty, Alaska, and a warm campfire. Isn't that what Alaska outdoors is all about anyway—friends, family, and a fire?

Sunken *Northwestern*

In Captain's Bay, on Unalaska Island, is the rusted hulk of the USS *Northwestern* poking its bow out of the water at the head of the bay. The *Northwestern* began service as an Alaska Steamship Company vessel in 1909. She had survived 16 groundings in the Inside Passage. Stationed at Dutch Harbor, the old ship had been driven ashore by a williwaw a few weeks before the June, 1942 Japanese attack. Two bombs scored direct hits on the deck of the beached ship, which was serving as a barracks for civilian construction workers. Then the Zeros strafed her. The resulting fires were brought under control by her dedicated deckhands, and she continued to serve the city for many months. Later the old ship was towed up to the head of Captain's Bay and scuttled.

Near the old USS *Northwestern*, the Shaishnikoff River empties into Captain's Bay. The Shaishnikoff originates in a small lake in the interior mountains about five miles inland. The lake is in a placid setting in the interior highlands. It sits in a bowl surrounded by small but rocky peaks that may be streaked with snow. Beyond the low rocky outcropping on the far side of the lake is the vast and wild expanse of the North Pacific Ocean.

Beginning at the old USS *Northwestern*, hiking to the lake is a straightforward, yet challenging hike. Unalaska is a hiker's paradise. There are no bears and no snakes on Unalaska Island.

Out on the chain, Unalaska doesn't have the spectacular, awe-inspiring beauty of the Alaska Range, the kind that assaults and overwhelms the visual sense. Here's a more subtle, refined, almost homey beauty that strikes right at the heart. From the old USS *Northwestern* to the snow-streaked mountains of Shaishnikoff Lake, it's easy to develop a love for the treeless terrain of the Aleutians.

Hunting is...

Once you pull the trigger, the fun is all over. If you need to shoot something to make a hunting trip successful, you went for the wrong reasons. I didn't ruin the hunt by killing something. These statements reflect an attitude expressed by hunters who come back skunked. In part they attempt to justify or rationalize the lack of game. Perhaps we have all used one or more of these excuses. I know I have. Looking back with a 40-year Alaska hunting perspective confirms that a truism was spoken each time such a statement was made.

Hunting is more than shooting. Talk to any hunter or search your own memory, and I'll bet it's the other things and not the shooting that made the hunt. It's the fireside at day's end, the northern lights shooting searchlight beams of color across a star-filled night sky, the full moon changing mountaintops from dark shadows to ice-white temple spires. It's campfire smoke in your eyes, blisters on your feet, bugs in your soup, and rocks under your sleeping bag. It's a rainbow after a storm, waking to the deafening silence of new snow, or just lying in your sleeping bag watching your breath on a cold morning.

It's not shooting that makes the hunt. It's not shooting that makes a person a hunter. He may have a scrapbook filled with photos or walls lined with trophies. He may own airplanes, boats, campers, and snow machines to get him afield. He may have hunted Africa, Asia, and Alaska. Rifles, shotguns, and pistols may fill his gun cabinet. He may have received awards, citations, and honors. Still it is the other things he remembers and speaks about.

Our family has its share of game in the freezer each winter. When the meat is prepared and dinner is served we remember, rehearse, and enlarge the size of the pack, the distance of the hike, and the quality of the cooking—not the shooting.

Hunting begins with the planning and the packing, the re-planning and the repacking. If the hunter goes for the wrong reasons, the hunt ends only when the trigger is pulled. Hunting success is not measured by the size or number of animals taken. It is measured by the sum of all the parts from concept to completion.

Maker of the Moose and Me

Just three months after his eleventh birthday, Easten took his first moose. It was an easy hunt, with just enough packing to make him realize that moose hunting is not all fun. Easten and his dad left their camp as dawn's first light burned the stars out of the clear sky. It was the first morning of their hunt.

In the half-light of morning the trail was difficult to follow and going was slow. An hour from their tent, they reached the east end of the swampy area they intended to watch, anticipating a traveling moose. By now, the sun had crested the eastern mountains and light flooded the snow-covered Alaska Range. Easten's dad asked him to walk ahead and pose for a picture. He moved 20 feet away and suddenly turned.

"Dad, there's a moose," he whispered, pointing to the western end of the mile-long swamp. Easten's sharp, young eyes saw the flash of white when the moose's antlers caught the sun. Both hunters moved to the edge of a patch of alders where they could see the moose without being seen themselves. The moose continued to advance up the opposite side of the swamp. A bullet was chambered in each rifle. It was obvious the animal was on a trail leading him to a spot 200 yards from where the hunters waited. Easten was told to shoot the moose when it got to a particular small swamp spruce. Moving slowly, the old moose took 30 minutes to progress to within 800 yards of the hunters.

From out of thick timber behind the moose, a challenging cry was heard. Easten's moose raised his head, received the call, and responded by moving off the trail and disappearing into the trees. Suddenly the swamp was empty. Minutes passed.

Then, charging out of the timber, a smaller moose, obviously in a hurry to escape the bigger animal, quickly moved up the trail formerly occupied by the big moose. As if by some pre-destined assignment, the moose moved to the 200-yard designated spot and stopped broadside. Easten raised his rifle and took his first big game animal.

In his youthful, inexperienced mind he thought this was the way all moose hunts ended, but his next hunting trip to Swensen's Lake proved to be less productive. During a week of hard hunting, only one moose, a cow, was spotted down the swamp a mile away.

Around the campfire on the last night, Easten asked, "What if we got up in the morning and a moose was standing right by the lake, could I shoot it?" He knew there wouldn't be time to leave camp and hunt and still be ready when Ketchum's Beaver came for the noon pickup. He didn't know that this was the last day of the hunting season.

"The season closes today," his dad informed him. "This is the last day we can legally hunt." Then, testing him, his dad asked, "If we got up early and one was standing right in camp and we shot it, who would know?"

Without hesitation Easten responded, "The Maker of the moose and me."

Those who violate fishing and hunting regulations and break the law in their sporting pursuits never escape, even if their crime is not solved by the authorities. They have to live with their guilt and knowledge that the Maker of the moose also knows. The next time a tempting opportunity to violate the law is present, I hope each of us will remember a 12-year-old boy's wise advice, "The Maker of the moose and me." I trust all outdoor experiences would be true recreation if this thought became part of every adult sportsman's ethics and he taught the young by example.

Mat Valley

The Valley is home to the Iditarod, footstool of Mt. McKinley and Denali National Park, and full of fun things for outdoor recreationists to do. People of all ages and persuasions come from Anchorage, Asia, America, and Europe to catch a king, climb a mountain, or snap a picture. Matanuska-Susitna Valley is where the dreams of many seekers of solitude, fish hunters, and mountain hikers come true.

The Valley, close to the state's largest population center, easily fits the description, "Alaska is minutes away from Anchorage." The Valley, bordered on the south by Matanuska and Knik Rivers, is surrounded by the Chugach and Talkeetna mountains, and the Alaska Range. It is bisected by glacier-fed, Susitna River which drains most of the Valley's tributaries into Cook Inlet.

The Matanuska-Susitna Valley takes its name from the two major rivers cutting across the flatlands beneath the mountains. Towering Mt. McKinley, North America's highest peak, watches over the Valley from the north. Melting, ageless glacier ice trickles from the slopes of McKinley's 20,300-foot summit. The trickles join together, gaining size as they cascade from the dizzy heights of their beginnings to the valley floor below. Larger streams are formed, some muddy with glacier silt, others clean and clear. Running water from McKinley marries with rivers and streams from the Chugach and Talkeetna Mountains to form the Susitna River.

Susitna, beginning on the slopes of McKinley, mixes with sea-level salt water as it terminates in a muddy delta in Cook Inlet. Through the delta, millions of migrating salmon move into Susitna to meet their fate as parents of orphans or at the end of an angler's line.

The area has been the scene of much mining activity and many trails follow paths taken by prospectors and supply trains. The Valley was introduced to modern settlers when, in 1935, the United States Government moved farmers from poverty-stricken Minnesota to Palmer and the surrounding region. Out of wilderness these homesteaders created a productive farming and dairy industry. Families of these homesteaders, new citizens, residents of Anchorage and other parts of the state, and visitors from outside use the Valley as a major recreation area.

The Matanuska-Susitna Valley is blessed with great beauty, clear, clean air, abundant wildlife, and outstanding fishing opportunities. Many Valley streams, accessible by road, may be crowded during the water's respective salmon runs, but the area is large, fishable waters are many, and road and water access easy.

There seems to be something pulling and tugging, making us want to go back to the days of '98—days when rugged men scratched the land in search of gold; days when the lucky struck it rich; days carefree and without constraints of traffic jams, television news updates, cellular telephones, and regular employment; days to wander where we will and see sights only we can see; days of closeness with the land; days where the supersonic speed of living is slowed to the pace of mist forming a dewdrop on the bottom of a red berry.

When Anchorage and its residents and those traveling from even bigger and faster, more unfriendly cities with traffic, television, telephones, and jobs, yearn to get away, when the craving strikes to leave it all, even if it's leaving for a moment, they can get into the outback in moments. The Matanuska-Susitna Valley can satisfy the urge and restore harmony to an unbalanced life.

Max Chickalusion

Max Chickalusion was an Alaska Native from Tyonek, and one of the best moose hunters and outdoorsmen I've known. My hunting trail ran into Max's moose-hunting camp one fall on the McAurther River on the west side of Cook Inlet.

Moose were scarce that season and our two hunting camps teamed up, pooled our resources, and hunted together. Max had an intimate knowledge of the hunting area, and I had a small boat we carried from the main river to a slough bisecting a superswamp whose timbered edges seemed to hold the area's only moose population.

A huge birch tree grew at the edge of the swamp that Max had visited many times before. The branches were so constructed as to allow a climber easy access from the ground to a semi-comfortable limb-chair in which a hunter could relax and spot game coming into the swamp.

Early one morning, Max took his old bolt action, military surplus 30:06 and climbed to his birch tree lookout. He hadn't been there too long when he whispered down to me that a big bull was starting to cross the swamp. Max gave him a few minutes to clear the trees and then brought his rifle to his shoulder. A morning breeze was blowing and the birch branches were slowly moving back and forth in response to the steady small wind.

I thought to myself, "Ain't nobody can shoot a moose from a moving tree at 400 yards. It'll be a wasted shot." I had hardly completed the thought when Max's gun reported that Max had more confidence in his shooting ability than I did. Three shots were fired in rapid succession: boom, boom,

boom. And, then Max climbed down. He was smiling when he reported, "I got him. Hit him three times."

Sure enough, Max's moose was stretched out on the only mound of dry ground for several hundred yards around, and he was within 10 feet of where we paddled our boat. It would make for an easy pack.

I'm an experienced hunter, but I sure got a doctorate degree in field dressing game as I assisted Max. His knife was half the size of mine, and I don't use a very big knife. All Max asked me to do was hold a leg here, move his antlers there, push on this side, etcetera, and in no time flat, the moose was freed of his skin and the entrails were out of the carcass. Max dug around in the gut pile and came up with a couple of parts he used as sacks to carry the heart and liver in. He took several other parts from the inside, as well as the tongue and nose. At one point, I jokingly ask Max which pile of guts we were taking and which pile we were leaving.

Max then turned to making the moose into sizes we could handle. Using his little knife, he knew just were to cut between joints and bones, and soon had nine smaller pieces of steaks and roasts ready to put in the boat.

As we were paddling back to the main river with our load of winter meat, I asked Max how many moose he had killed. He looked off into the distance in deep thought and then turning, he replied "God only know."

Mush You Huskies

I've seen every World Championship Dog Race for the last four decades. Mushing for me was a spectator sport before I met Fred Agree. On our first meeting, Fred invited me on a dog-mushing trip. One Friday in late March I decided to take Agree up on the invitation. The day was warm. The weather the whole week suggested spring was just around the corner. The desire to get out had infected me and by Friday I was on the critical list. Remembering Agree's invitation, it seemed like a proper prescription. RX: "Take thou this." The cure was only a telephone call away.

Fred said he would be glad to take me and my son Lars for a ride. "Bring your camera and come for breakfast so we can get an early start." I quit playing golf when my buddies kept insisting on 6 a.m. tee times. I've been trying to organize the fishing guide union into mandatory 9 a.m. wake-up calls. Now this dog driver wants to get an early start. It was, however, this telephone call that convinced me dog mushers have a different relationship with time as Fred said, "Be here between 9:00 and 9:30 for breakfast." I wondered if he played golf or was interested in being a fishing guide.

Forty dogs howled a welcome as we turned off the highway and came down the drive to Agree's place. The noise must have signaled our arrival long before we could see the house, for Agree was waiting in the doorway when we pulled in.

Fred Agree looks like a musher. He wears shoe packs on the end closest to the ground and a salt-and-pepper beard on the other. As with most mushers, his uniform consists of wool pants and a shirt sprinkled with traces of dog hair.

While we were eating our breakfast one of the kennel's

handlers loaded the team and all the gear into a truck. Because the snow was too sparse and wet on the trails nearby, we trucked to the higher altitude of Hatcher Pass.

Fred's dogs are gentle, obedient, and well mannered. As soon as the sleds were removed from the top of the truck, we began unloading the dogs.

I guess for the same reason the biggest kid in school is called tiny, Agree's pure white leader is named Blackie. Blackie, the first dog out, was turned loose to roam around while the other dogs were unloaded. Fred explained the extra privileges make the dog feel like a leader and he gains respect from the other dogs. They accept his leadership and he then maintains control of the rest of the team.

We unloaded the other dogs from their boxes and tied them close to the truck. Fred whistled for Blackie, who came running, anxious to take his place at the top of the line. Once in place, Blackie pulled the line tight and maintained order until all the dogs were hooked up.

A couple of the dogs acted up and Fred bit their ears, making them yelp. Fred explained he never bites hard enough to really hurt. He claimed it embarrasses the dogs to cry out and they shape up. It seemed to work.

\By experience, Blackie knew when everything was ready and it was time to go. He began jumping and pulling, trying to get the sled to move. I was instructed to get into the sled. Lars got in the sled driven by the handler. Fred pulled the brakes and with a gentle "Hike," we were off down the trail. The dog's feet flipped snow in my face like small tires spinning to get traction. The noise of the sled runners sliding over the snow, propelled by eleven sets of feet, was the only sound to break the stillness. Dogs are directed by verbal commands. Gee and Haw for turning and naturally, Whoa for stop.

We topped a small hill and Fred yelled, "Whoa." This was where we rested the dogs, took in the view, and changed drivers. Mt. McKinley was directly ahead. We were separated from the highest mountain in North America by 150 miles of wilderness. Even at that distance, the 20,300-foot high mountain looked enormous.

Fred and the handler got into the sleds and Lars and I became mushers. Not only did the ride take us into the backcountry, but I imagined I was back in history to the days of the gold rush and the trapper. Before I knew it, we were back at the cabin and it was time to come back to the 20th century and go home.

During the drive back home, Lars said he enjoyed handling the dogs. He told me the most impressive thing about the day was Fred's knowledge and quiet manner with the animals. He was surprised that obedience existed even in a pack. The most fun, of course, was standing on the runners and driving his own team.

Litter

Why is it that some otherwise caring, intelligent, and thoughtful people are such litterbugs? Take some smokers for example. Insensitive as a common barnyard animal, they dispose of the waste of their habit. Cigarette butts are dropped on trails, thrown on sidewalks, and tossed out car windows. The very people who would not even think of throwing a gum wrapper out, will roll down their car window at a stoplight and toss a cigarette butt on the pavement.

They empty their automobile ashtray where it pleases them, in the supermarket parking lot or on the public campground. The countryside is tainted by their lack of common consideration. Somehow they need to learn the remains of their habit is litter and should be disposed of properly, the same as any other garbage.

Akin to the smoker is the beer and soda pop drinker. Beer cans and soda pop bottles line the sides of roads, trails, and highways. Waysides, campgrounds, and favorite fishing spots reflect the drinker's thoughtless acts. Not all offenders are outdoorsmen, but too many are.

If you are one of those who litter, stop immediately. You are fouling your own nest. Think for just a moment how your thoughtless actions spoil the outdoor experience of others. You unknowingly lessen the experience for yourself and for those who accompany you. Think what you are teaching the young in your care or under your influence. Even your fishing buddies are ashamed of you.

Other offenders are the State Parks and Recreation people who are responsible for the wayside and campground litter stations. Why are the cans left too long between pickups? Almost all the areas around these cans are strewn with litter blown from overfilled cans. Even the garbage of thoughtful and caring outdoorsmen and travelers ends up soiling and spoiling the scene.

If you are a witness to littering, report it to the proper authority. Get names, license numbers, and photographs. Let's get tough on those who litter. Let them know littering is not an accepted part of the outdoor experience. Those insisting on dumping their trash and garbage on the highways and byways should be ostracized from the outdoors. Those who are offended by such actions need to speak up and make it plain that leaving the campsite with trash, throwing cigarette butts to the wind, and tossing beer cans and other garbage along the highways and riverbanks will not be tolerated. If we don't stop it now, many places will not be fit to visit.

I observed a group of fishermen from Japan fishing the Talachulitna River recently. Several of the group were smokers. Those who were carried a small ashtray attached to their fly vests. They not only refrained from throwing their cigarette butts into the water, the ashes went into ashtrays as well.

Most guides I fish with spend part of each day picking up litter left by less thoughtful outdoorsmen. One group of Anchorage boaters spends one weekend a year cleaning up the banks of the upper Deshka River. Litter left for the most part by resident Alaskan boaters, campers, and fishermen.

Other thoughtless people who seem to crop up at recreation sites are the polluters; polluters of the air with loud, obnoxious yelling, ghetto blasters turned to maximum volume, and profane language that would embarrass a mule skinner. This type of behavior has no place on the riverbank.

I was taught in my learning years that "profanity was an attempt of a lazy and feeble mind to express itself forcibly." Profanity and vulgar language are out of place at any time, but they particularly offend the senses in the outdoors. Those who enjoy the base must learn to keep it away from women, young people, and others of sensitive spirit.

The outdoors is the handiwork of the Creator. We are the stewards of that creation. It is up to us to enjoy, preserve, and leave it better for future generations. The way it is going, we are using it more, enjoying it less, and destroying it for ourselves and those who follow. A gum wrapper, a beer can, a cigarette butt, a vulgar remark, loud shouting, or any other litter, garbage, or pollution lessens the recreation experience of any who see or hear. Each of us is either part of the problem or part of the solution. Which are you?

Play Together, Stay Together

Bob pulled the plug on the boat, tilted it so any water that got in would run out, and covered it with canvas. As he was putting on the canvas, his neighbor, Jim, came out and offered to help. Together they completed the task of securing the boat against winter elements and were standing around shooting the breeze.

The light conversation suddenly turned serious when Jim asked, "You know, Bob, I know you've got the same number of kids I do. You make about the same money and I think your house payment should be similar to mine. What I'd like to know is how you do it. You guys have a boat, we don't. You've got a garage full of ski equipment and you'll be on the slopes Saturdays now that you've put the boat away. It costs a bunch of money for equipment and lift tickets. Money we can't afford, but you do. How can your family afford to do all these things together and ours can't?"

Being good friends and knowing Jim was serious and wanted an honest answer, Bob replied. "The only thing I can think of is, you've done a lot of remodeling in your house over the years. Last summer you put in a new bathroom. We wanted to remodel our old bathroom, but decided on getting ski equipment instead."

Bob continued, "Last year our oldest son Mark went off to college. He'd been gone for a couple of months and was getting homesick. His letters reflected his feelings. One day, about Thanksgiving time, we got a letter from Mark. He told us how he loved and missed his family. Then he reminded us about the good times we'd had together out on the slopes and with the boat. At the end of the letter, he said, 'Dad, thanks for taking me skiing and fishing. We've really had a good time together as a family.'"

I doubt Mark would write home and tell Bob how wonderful the new bathroom was. In the pursuit to get things, we need to put things in a proper perspective. Fathers need to spend time with their children, not buy them things. Not time in front of the television or behind the daily newspaper, but time doing the things the youngsters want to do. Most young people will be more receptive to receiving the lessons of work, honesty, integrity, and the other qualities it takes for them to become the citizens you want them to be, if you give them your time—time in the outdoors learning outdoor lessons, but also the lessons of life.

It has been said that a father who hunts with his child when he is young, will not have to hunt for him when he is old. I think I'd add fishing, boating, hiking, picnicking, skiing, or any other outdoor adventure. Give your kids everything. Give them your time.

Charles Francis Adams, grandfather of the second president of the United States, was a successful lawyer, a member of the U.S. House of Representatives, and the U.S. Ambassador to Britain. Amidst his responsibilities, he had little time to spare. He did, however, keep a diary. One day he wrote, "Went fishing with my son today—a day wasted!"

On that same date, Charles' son, Brook Adams, printed in his own diary, "Went fishing with my father today—the most wonderful day of my life."

Fathers and mothers, take your sons and daughters afield. See if they don't write in their diary, "Went fishing with my Dad, the most wonderful day of my life."

Straight Stretch

We were driving north from Seattle. It was the trip back home after an extended stay in the South 48. Ahead, we noticed road construction signs and alerted ourselves to possible changes. It began to rain early in the afternoon and soon the surface of the gravel road turned to mud. Construction signs became more frequent and the road dissolved into muck, ruts, and rocks. Entering an area of steep hills, deep valleys, and a twisting, turning road, we were forced to reduce our speed to 15 miles an hour. Constant road signs read: *Bump, Slow, Steep Hill, Check Your Brakes, Sharp Curve, Slow Down, Go Slow, Keep Headlights On.* At one point we battled up a long graded hill, muck to our hubcaps, and mud splashing from beneath the tires covered our windows. The road and construction signs were fast becoming victorious. We could see the top of the grade, but had little hope for improved conditions. We were worn out.

At the top of the hill the road appeared, paved, straight, and stretching into a distant unspoiled beauty. What a surprise. Coming into our view was a large handmade sign, spray-painted on a piece of plywood by a construction worker: STRAIGHT STRETCH, GIVE HER HELL. We broke into a laugh.

That trip was in the early 1960s. We have told the story of the *Straight Stretch, Give Her Hell* sign. It always draws a laugh. In those days we carried extra tires, fan belts, tools, extra gas, emergency clothing, and food. We protected the headlights, covered the grill and radiator with a screen, and placed a piece of rubber over the gas tank. We knew repair work in Canada could take from one to ten days, depending on shipping time from the United States. The prices of parts and service were out of sight.

Today's Alaska Highway is probably the finest gravel road in the world and much of it is paved. The Canadians have developed a way to mix ground-up tires and mud to give the road many of the characteristics of blacktop. The mud holes and constant dust have been practically eliminated. Modern camper parks and repair services are available at reasonable prices and regular intervals along the road. The people operating visitor services are helpful and friendly to the extreme.

Today's Alaska Highway adventurer can go home with more wild and exciting tales than mud, bugs, and potholes. Side roads have opened fishing, camping, hunting, sightseeing, and other outdoor recreation possibilities. You can go back 100 years in 20 miles and return to blacktop the same day.

Since that trip in the 60s, we've been over the Alaska Highway more than 25 times. Each time seems to be better than the last, but it is still a long trip. Since our first trip, we coined a phrase to describe the Alaska Highway. We said it was "lots and lots of miles and miles." And that is exactly what it is— look, a straight stretch, give her hell!

Take a Kid Hunting

Outdoor outings provide many teaching moments when you take a kid along. Your children learn your values, and you may even learn from your children. Such was the case when my 13-year-old son, Lars, and I were moose hunting in the Alaska Range.

It was the last week of the season and it was raining mixed with snow. It was Lars's first moose hunt. We left camp before daylight and hiked to a low hill where we could watch a long, narrow, swampy area. As daylight progressed the rain and snow intensified and the temperature dropped. We spent a couple of cold, wet, miserable hours.

Finally Lars stood up to stretch his legs and get his blood circulating again. As he stood and turned to look behind us he discovered a big bull moose had slipped in and was staring our way.

"Dad, Dad," he whispered, "there's a moose. A moose standing right there." Our scopes were set on nine power as we watched the swamp, knowing that any shot we might have an opportunity to take would be more than 200 yards. As we both turned our rifles toward the moose, the rain mixed with snow magnified in the scope's lens caused the moose to be just a hazy outline. It took a moment for us to adjust, but the moose just stood broadside and made no attempt to flee. With the crack of the rifle our hunt was over and the hard work commenced.

I got out the tools to begin dressing out our winter's meat supply. Lars stopped me before I got started and said, "Dad let's kneel down here and thank Heavenly Father for providing our family with this moose." As we knelt in the snow and rain, and I heard my son talk to his Father in Heaven, I silently gave thanks for my son.

Yes, outdoor outings do provide many teaching moments when you take a kid along. Your children learn your values and, you may even learn from your children. Such was the case when my 13 year old son and I were moose hunting in the Alaska Range. For that winter, each time we had moose meat for dinner or in a sandwich, I remembered the lesson I learned because I had taken a kid hunting.

Don't Kill the Dream

by Lars Swensen

Stepping back toward my tent, I half-turned and noticed two caribou spying on my camp. They froze. The only thing moving was their breath condensing and leaking from their wet noses. Glancing up I saw the two silent figures push back the forest-trapped fog, and disappear.

Fog gave way just enough for me to see the rise from which I wanted to spot. There, in a sunburnt opening on my hill, was a large white-cuffed caribou. Midmorning rays beat down on his velvet-free antlers. My heart pounded so loud I knew for certain the antler-clad mammoth standing firmly on the hill could hear. I reached for my gun.

His mighty antlers split the light fog. I could see the protruding rack hang in the air, moving slowly away, teasing me until it fell out of sight and he disappeared over the rise. The hill where he once stood was about a hundred yards away. Could I climb it in time to get a second chance at the trophy?

Reaching the top of the hill, my eyes frantically searched for my challenge. It felt like my heart would explode any minute with excitement. Sitting down did not help nor did it slow the beating in my chest. It did give me time to contemplate the size and beauty of this heavy-chested caribou.

The sun broke through the morning fog, and I could see the area. "There, behind that large patch of alder," my mind shouted to me. "The white hind end of a very large caribou!" He quickly stepped deeper into the cover, less than 150 yards away. I didn't have a clear shot unless he left the thicket. I couldn't see him; however, I knew he was there.

He pushed his mighty rack out beyond the edge of the

alder patch and the sight urged massive rushes of air into my already overworked lungs. I watched him slowly move closer and closer. The caribou froze broadside to me. He knew I was there and could smell the human odor. Filling the optics with white hair, cross hairs set perfectly, I watched in the calm sunlight. He lifted his large wood-like rack, tensely holding his breath, ready for flight.

My moistened finger wrapped softly around the cold steel trigger; I could feel the pressure building up inside the chamber. The loud roar of thunder awoke me.

After a few moments of empty attempts at sleep, I decided to go outside. Pushing on my night-cold boots and grabbing my rifle, I quietly unzipped the door. Something caught my eye as I turned. Right behind my tent stood a large caribou. His antlers rose high into the frosty air. His hot breath bellowed from deep inside a white chest.

My heart jumped with excitement. Slinging my gun into firing position, the scope instantly filled with thick hair. Left eye shut, my right eye laid the cross hairs right under his shoulder blade. Time stood still, sounds were gone and feeling left my body. I opened my left eye to see the whole animal once more. Thoughts of how large his rack was and how beautiful a trophy he would make rushed through my mind.

As I paused again to aim carefully, something came over me. I slowly lowered my rifle and sighed softly. I didn't want to shoot something I had dreamt about. I put the leather strap over my shoulder and without regret, watched the caribou move away over the hill.

A Majority of One

Several years ago we published an editorial taking the Anchorage Convention and Visitors Bureau to task for what we thought was misleading advertising. Their ads, placed in national publications, gave readers the impression they could fish for king salmon in downtown Anchorage, view eagles and caribou from their hotel room window, walk to a glacier on the way to the restaurant, and Mt. McKinley was an Anchorage landmark.

Some of those engaged in the visitor and tourist industry challenged us for discouraging the Bureau. They pointed out the ad campaign had won awards in the advertising community and was good for business. In their minds, if it was good business and worthy of artistic awards the lie was justified. We received very strong letters from some industry leaders. Several even canceled their advertising contract with us.

The very next year the Bureau's advertising thrust was cleaned up and a more honest approach was taken. They developed the theme of "In town, around town, and out of town," which more truthfully portrayed the location of attractions. The resulting advertising was superior to the former and it did not burden the local service provider with the responsibility of defending an ill-conceived promotion program.

Later, the very ones who were most vocal in defending the misleading ad campaign withdrew their membership from the Bureau and called for the resignation of its president. The president withdrew and the organization seems to have corrected their weaknesses and are doing a reliable, honest, honorable, and aggressive job of promoting Anchorage. More and more visitors and conventions are coming to the city.

They come with realistic expectations of what is here and go away happy.

Since its conception, the State of Alaska Division of Tourism has spent its advertising dollars supporting non-Alaskans. Their advertising has been centered on activities, and aimed at a segment of the population supporting firms whose home offices are outside the state. Like the ad with the scantily clad young lady posing on a Mt. McKinley glacier, some of their ads have been misleading, some even dishonest. We took exception to this in an editorial and again suffered heat and lost revenues from those who saw no wrong in spending the state's money at the expense of its citizenry.

With the coming of new leadership in the Department of Economical Development and Division of Tourism we hoped for and were promised new direction that supported Alaskans. Concurrent with new leadership state revenues went down and politicians began calling it hard times. Those signing the check began to say that they would let the non-Alaskans support their own advertising and the state would develop programs helping hometown business.

After 8 years of promises little if anything has been done to assist Alaskans in promoting, marketing, and developing a homegrown visitor and tourism industry. Progress has been made by many individual companies without help and direction from state agencies. The same outside operations the last two administrations said they would not support in conflict with local business now sit on the boards that control where, when, and in what market segment the state's advertising money is spent. They are stronger and more in control than ever before.

We don't claim to be the only ones who assisted the Anchorage Convention and Visitors Bureau to correct their portrayed image, but we helped. Sometimes a lone voice can be a majority of one.

Enough and to Spare

I've read newspaper and magazine articles, viewed videos and movies, received news releases and announcements, and heard radio monologues about our tender environment. Almost always they tell and show some species of animal or plant or area of the earth that's in trouble. Invariably the material will depict man as an evil passenger on the planet. They cry big alligator tears for the real or imagined loss of a given flora or fauna. Many times they point out the number of species man has been responsible for obliterating out of existence. They even get down to how many are being lost per hour. They are the masters of manipulating numbers to make their point.

Several things seem to be missing in their message (generally followed by a solicitation for money). First, they fail to recognize the trillions of plants and animals that left the planet before man entered the scene. Nearly all, if not all, of our so-called nonrenewable resources are the remains of plant and animal species that became extinct prior to the time of man. The coming and going of life has been here since the designer and Creator of our world put this sphere in its place in the heavens.

Had the protectors of the planet been around in the days of the dinosaur, they would have attempted to save the dinosaur, the purposes of the Creator would have been frustrated, we'd be without energy, and man would have ceased to exist. And, that's the second thing. They give schooled and knowledgeable explanations of the demise of a snail or a bug, and follow with the attendant big tears. In practically the same breath they tell of a recent, in terms of the world's history, lost civilization of man. But, no tears for the loss of the species to which the tellers of the tale belong. They just grab up their lance and charge after another environmental windmill.

When it comes to Alaska, usually they're the latecomers who also want to protect Alaska from Alaskans. They're the first to cry jobs for Alaskans first, but the last to preach Alaska for Alaskans. They want the jobs and the big money, but they don't seem to want Alaskans to enjoy Alaska. And, if they do, it's usually on their New York and Washington D.C. terms which ofttimes exclude Alaskans who moved here and pioneered the wilderness so the protesters could come and be warm and comfortable in their protesting and fund-raising.

My attitude is, we don't care how they do it Outside, or how the Outsiders want it done in Alaska. For me, it's first—Alaska for Alaskans.

I'm grateful that we've arrived at the point that we're better stewards of our God-given resources. And that brings up my third observation. Doesn't anybody ever do anything right? Isn't there at least one evil capitalistic company out there doing most things right? Surely one man on earth is as concerned for the environment as the requester of funds. Not to hear them tell it. We're all bad, and they've got to protect everything that's not homo sapiens from homo sapiens.

In their zeal, if we let them, they'll protect man right out of existence. We can only hope that the haters of man will be the first to go. Once they're gone, maybe those left can live in peace and in harmony with each other and with the Creator who said, "Behold, there is enough and to spare."

How Is it Really

A few years ago I was with an Alaska company as an exhibitor at the Houston, Texas Sports and Travel Show. We had been careful in choosing our material and did not include anything if it had even a hint of snow or ice. We were anxious to put our best summer foot forward.

During the course of the show two schoolteachers approached the booth and greeted us with enthusiasm. They explained that their classes had been studying Alaska the past several days and wondered if we had any interesting material they could take back to school to share with their students. We loaded them up with publications, and filled their shopping bags with brochures and videos.

Upon their departure they thanked us graciously and prepared to leave. After taking a few steps into the aisle, one of them returned. In a quiet voice, almost a whisper, she asked, "Is it really cold, dark, and snowy there all the time?"

Almost every call or letter our family receives contains a weather report inquiry. Is it really cold? Do you have snow? What is the temperature? People seem to refuse to believe the truth. Prior to Mom's first visit to Alaska, she was victim of these misconceptions. Late one May I was in her home in Salt Lake City. Almost concurrent with questions concerning mutual acquaintances, she asked about the present weather. I told her of our pleasant, warm, long days and about our garden preparation. After courteously listening, she leaned forward and whispered so no one else could hear, "I know, but how is it—really?"

I told her it was 50 degrees below zero, the snow had melted down to where we could now see out of the top half of the windows at home, and we expected the sun again in a few weeks. Sitting back in her chair, she smugly exclaimed, "That's just what I thought."

That's what too many people think. Even in the face of hard evidence to the contrary, they persist in believing the misconceptions. It appears to be easier to retell the myths than accept the truth. I've wondered if those two Texas schoolteachers don't represent part of the reason these false impressions continue. Unless I miss my guess, their students did not get a true picture of Alaska and probably will grow up thinking Seward's Folly is nothing but icebergs and glaciers. Even with today's storehouse of information in print, on videos, and on television, a lot of people still think Alaska is synonymous with North Pole and Antarctica.

Mom's spent a few summers in Anchorage, and even some winter time, and is now a frustrated Alaska goodwill emissary. "Why," she asks, "do people think it's always cold, dark, and snowy?"

I don't know. Maybe they don't get the newspaper. Perhaps their schoolteacher taught them, or possibly they listen to their Mom, before she came to Alaska to thaw out.

It's Alaska, Not Alaskan

Suppose you lived in California and read a headline in the *Los Angeles Times'* outdoor section: Californian Offshore Fishing Improves. What would a Utah deer hunter think if the *Salt Lake Tribune* used Utahn Deer in their hunting report? An eastern outdoor editor is not likely to write about New Yorker trout fishing any more than the *Los Angeles Times* will use Californian fishing, or the *Salt Lake Tribune* will refer to Utahn deer.

Pick up any Alaska newspaper or almost any publication with a reference to Alaska's outdoors, its wildlife, or its fish and you will read Alaskan this and Alaskan that. It is not an Alaskan trout any more than it is a Californian trout. I wish the purveyors of printed material would stop misusing Alaskan. An Alaskan is a person. Alaskan is not a trout, a moose, a trip, or even an adventure.

Alaskan has been used incorrectly for so long by so many that it has nearly become acceptable. Pick up the *Anchorage Daily News* or *Alaska* magazine and you can hardly read a page where the error is not perpetuated. Writers write and editors continue to permit the error. You can even witness this abuse in the names of shops, stores, and other businesses.

This is one Alaskan who knows the difference. When I'm in the outdoors, I'll seek Alaska caribou and Alaska moose. I'll fly out in an Alaska floatplane, land on an Alaska lake, pitch my tent on Alaska soil, and watch an Alaska sun set and an Alaska moon rise. I'll take photographs and write about my Alaska adventure. Some of the photographs and stories will be published in *Alaska Outdoors*. For certain, I'm not going to shoot an Alaskan moose or caribou. It won't be an Alaskan sunset I watch and it won't be an Alaskan moon rising over the Alaskan Range, and I won't have an Alaskan adventure.

You can bet your poke we never even considered calling our radio program "Alaskan Outdoors Radio Magazine," or the magazine, *Alaskan Outdoors*.

Motoring Up Memories
by Lars Swensen

Jeff Penman turned off his machine's motor and slowly stood on the foot pegs. Putting his hand to his brow like a Cherokee scout, he said, "Lars this is the end of our trail. Let's camp for the night."

Jeff dismounted like a cowboy off a trail horse after a month-long cattle drive. Playing up the act, he walked around bow-legged for the first minutes. For a moment, I expected him to start talking like John Wayne.

Jeff started a fire. I set up our nylon Hilton. Smells and sounds of setting up camp grabbed many forgotten memories stored in my hair-covered hard drive. "Jeff, remember when you and I stayed a week on the Talachulitna River?" I asked while snapping on our tent's rain fly.

Jeff nodded, still hunched over the fire blowing slowly on the glowing embers, trying to get a flame. For some reason, on every trip since Jeff and I were 10 years old, he was always in charge of starting the fire.

"And when we heard a bear, we took off running down the trail, tripping and falling the whole way to the lodge," I said, delighted by the childhood remembrance.

He sat up, leaned back on his boots, and laughed out loud. "When we got to the lodge, we kept pulling the wrong way on the door thinking we were locked out and the bear was going to eat us."

I knew exactly what he was talking about. I sat on my ATV and held my sides, imagining two boys running for their lives, tripping and stumbling and getting to the lodge, only to pull the wrong direction on the door. The funniest part is the growl we heard was most likely a jet flying overhead. Then, we thought it was a bloodthirsty bear hungering for us.

Mountains rose above the sun and shadows crept toward us. Our campfire's glow sent orange streaks short distances through the twisted woodland, pushing back whiskers of darkness.

"I'm going to wander off to bed now," I told Jeff. Using two shirts and my jacket for a pillow, I snuggled my head all the way to the ear lobes. Pre-sleep thoughts started to come before I rolled over and went to sleep.

I have been hunting, fishing, and growing up with Jeff for most of my life. As kids we chased monster boats swallowing 30-foot king salmon in Campbell Lake, shot at werewolves with BB guns, and even mowed lawns for spending money. Yet this trip is the most memorable because it was our last.

Except for semiannual phone calls, I have not heard from Jeff. We no longer spin childhood dreams together around a campfire as we once did, but we are closer in some ways than ever before. He is married, has children. I am married and have two kids. The childlike adventures I participate in are now with my sons. Every time my boys and I make a fort out of blankets and pillows, playing hide-and-seek, or ride on ATV, reminds me of Jeff Penman. In this way we will always be good friends. In this way we will always be those two boys running for the lodge on the Talachulitna.

The Last Hunt

Each of us probably has hunting partners who have moved, lost interest, become incapacitated, or passed away. The memory of our last hunting trip with them has become very special. Whomever we hunt with, whether it be family, friends, or business associates, one of our hunts with them will be our last. It may be we who move, cannot go afield because of physical conditions, or die. One of our hunts will be our last hunt and the memory will become very important to us or to someone.

Because our next trip may be our last trip, we need to be sure we go hunting for the right reasons and leave the right memories. The right reason, unless we live a subsistence lifestyle, is never to go just to kill something. Ask any hunter, or examine your own hunting experiences, and you will find the most pleasant memories of any outing had nothing to do with taking an animal. It's the other things that make a hunt, from preparation to putting the gun away.

Occasionally, I talk to people who went for the wrong reason. The success of their hunting trip was predicated on killing an animal. If they got their game, it was a good trip. If they came home skunked, it was a bad one. All their enjoyment was keyed to bringing home a trophy, whether it be horns, antlers, or meat. Something to hang on the wall or a photo of a dead animal for their slide show makes the difference between having a good time or bad.

Their motivation for being outdoors so dominates their thinking, they forget to have fun. Sometimes they create their own bad trip by their attitude. Unfortunately, because they went for the wrong reasons, they soil or spoil other hunters' outdoor time by things they do and say.

Those who go for the right reasons have a good time in spite of weather or amount of game. They respect other hunters, those in their own party or strangers sharing the area, and treat them and the outdoors with thoughtfulness and respect. They pick up their litter and leave a clean camp. Hunters following them never find carelessly tossed gum wrappers or cigarette butts to mar their trip and scar the countryside. They don't mix gunpowder and alcohol. They are nonpolluters. They are courteous to other hunters. They are considerate of nonhunters. They're not loud. They don't shoot garbage cans and road signs. They have a deep respect for the Creator's creations. They treat the hunting area like a fine lady and other hunters like important strangers.

In an issue of *Alaska Outdoors* Jim Alleman shared his most recent moose hunt with us. He and his partners, Tom Kreuger, Curly Gere, and Harvey Otto, had a very productive hunt, but I suspect their trip would have been fulfilling had they not been so lucky to find a moose pasture.

Because of a mix-up in communication, the first-timer in the group of otherwise seasoned hunters committed a breach of outdoor etiquette. After the experienced hunters stalked a moose to within easy bow-and-arrow range, their new hunting partner shot the trophy bull with a rifle. Instead of being angry and ruining their own hunt and his, they made him the brunt of friendly campfire ribbing. They preserved their relationship, kept a proper perspective of why modern men hunt, and thus preserved their hunting experience.

Further evidence of this group's attitude of going for the right reasons was their consideration for one of the party who became ill. They insured he was a part of the activity even when he was too sick to leave camp. In addition, they allowed the first-timer to take the group's only caribou and brown bear. Not only did they allow it, they promoted it.

I suspect they will be talking about this hunt for an awfully long time. More than the trophies and meat they brought home, I'll bet the conversations will be friendly stories about Harvey shooting over their heads and The Tractor "shirking" his packing duties. They went for the right reasons and even when things didn't go right, it didn't spoil their adventure. Lesser men would have got mad at another's error and complained about a sick friend's bad luck. In so doing they would have fouled their own outing and created bad memories of what could turn out to be the group's last hunt together.

We hope the Jim Alleman group gets to go again and again, that Harvey's first hunt is just one in a row, and The Tractor gets a chance to live up to his nickname. Whatever is down the road for them, or which hunt will actually be their last, we can't say. We know it will be a great time because we know their group goes for the right reasons.

Those who go for the right reasons always fill their expectations, even when they don't fill their tag. Every trip, even when they come home skunked, is a memory producer. If their recent outing was their last outing, they'd have no regrets.

I hope your next hunting excursion isn't your last. If it is, and one of them will be, I hope it's your best even if you don't fill your license. I trust you will have the most happiest memories of your last trip.

One Last Cast

I have the best job in the world. I get up in the morning, pick up my fishing rod, kiss my wife goodbye, tell her I'm going to work—and she believes me!

Fishing and recreating in Alaska outdoors has been my vocation, but sometimes it's just hard work—not unpleasant work—but work. There are times when I'd like to leave my camera in the boat or escape from the TV camera's glaring eye for a moment and be alone with the wilderness and just go fishing.

One such time happened on the Togiak River. There was a lull in filming and I walked about a quarter mile up an incoming, clear-water side stream. On the second or third cast, a 5-pound rainbow yielded to my offering. Alone with my fish and the river in Alaska's wilderness, I played the trout as best I could and thrilled to the tug-of-war battle. It was a great fight, especially since it was just me and the fish, and no director telling me to "play to the camera."

Eventually the fish gave out and I prepared to release it. Then, I remembered my film crew downstream—back to work, Evan. I allowed the fish to gain fast water and it quickly, in typical rainbow fashion, with me in tow, took off for the Togiak. As the fish entered the main river I called, "Fish on!" and cameras started rolling. We filmed, what to the viewing audience appeared as the catch and release of a big 'bow. The two-minute segment ended one of Alaska Outdoors TV programs. The off-camera voice introduced the segment with "There's just time for one last cast." The show ends as the fish is released. With its release an idea was born and Alaska Outdoors Radio Magazine had a new ending for each day's program and the title of this book came into being.

I often think about the one-last-cast rainbow and wish every fishing outing ended in a similar way. I guess we'll end this book that way—there's just time for one last cast. It's your turn. Go ahead and cast.